HARD OPEN

THE COST OF MISTAKES

JEFF LEWIS

 FriesenPress

One Printers Way
Altona, MB R0G 0B0
Canada

www.friesenpress.com

Editors: Judie Land & Marc Hodgkinson

ISBN
978-1-03-911562-0 (Hardcover)
978-1-03-911561-3 (Paperback)
978-1-03-911563-7 (eBook)

Business & Economics, Entrepreneurship

Distributed to the trade by The Ingram Book Company

TABLE OF CONTENTS

DEDICATION

I dedicate this book to my wife Lynette, I'm sorry for the financial and emotional stress I caused and the uncertainty that followed. Without your love and support I don't believe I would have been able to get out of the emotional and psychological state I was in.

To my daughters, Stella and Grace. You're my daily motivation to be a better person, and strive to meet my potential as a provider and father. I love you both more than words can describe.

To my Father. Thank you for instilling your knowledge and loyalty in me.

Thank you my parents, Patricia Lewis-Taylor and Bill Taylor. The faith and support you provide me is immeasurable, and very appreciated.

I want to thank my mother and father-in-law, Bob and Martha Heywood for your help in a time I had no where else to turn and keeping me from being ruined.

Thanks to my mother and father in-law, Scott Rowland and Kathy Heywood for always helping, providing advice, and giving us much needed breaks as parents during these stressful times.

Thanks to my Uncle Mike Avery for the precise renovation work. Without you, I would be a ship without a dock.

Thanks to my Uncle Bill Avery. Your blind trust in me is something I will never forget.

Thank you Lya Brown for introducing me to Judie Land Smith, my first editor. Thank you Judie for your time, expertise, and providing me with such great direction to complete this book.

I want to thank my staff, Julie Jariott, Lorna MacDougal, and Daniel Gemmell. Your dedication, hard work, and faith that we would get through this is a major reason why came out on the other side.

Lastly, to my friend Marc Hodgkinson. Thank you for the literary guidance throughout this process, and for being a great friend and my personal therapist as I negotiate each stage in life.

PROLOGUE

NEVER SELL YOUR NAME

On February 7, 1990, I woke up from a deep sleep; my mother was standing beside mine and my brother's bunk bed. It was the coldest, most bitter winter morning I have ever experienced, although it was a clear, sunny day. I looked at my mother to hear the words, "There is nothing more they can do," and in an instant, my life was forever changed. Hearing those words caused more pain in that split second than I ever thought was possible for a human to feel. I wandered through my house in a daze, observing my mother, brother, and sisters, challenged to make this day appear normal and to make sense of our new reality. I was in grade six, seven weeks away from my twelfth birthday, and I had just learned that my father had passed away during the night. After receiving the news, my first instinct was to go about my day as if nothing had happened. I forced my mom to make arrangements to get me to school. As I was driven to school—up Highway 8 from Sebringville, Ontario, to Stratford, where my school was located—I watched the snow drift across the empty fields.

When I got to my classroom, I could feel my classmates' eyes on me, knowing what had just happened. They were scared to say anything to me at all. I sat quietly at my desk, staring out into the sky as memories and images of my father flitted in and out of my mind. The little things came to mind: from getting home from school, getting off the bus and coming into the house to find my dad trying to break our Atari scores on various games; to Dad wrestling with me; singing in the morning in his tighty-whities; letting me steer the car as he pretended to sleep while driving in the country; to the two of us swimming in our unfinished pool on his days off while my older siblings were in school and the youngest was sleeping.

I was confused as to why this had happened to us and wondered, what would we do now? How would anything ever seem or be normal again? I was angry, I was sad, and, for the first time, even knowing I had aunts and uncles, cousins, friends, and my immediate family beside me, I felt completely alone. One thought continually passed through my mind, and, like a sharp knife, cut deeper with each pass: the last thing I remembered saying to my dad was that I hated him. I'm sure now that wasn't actually the last thing I said, but it is definitely the last thing I remember saying, and it was the furthest thing from the truth. I had spoken out of childish and selfish anger over something trivial, and I didn't even remember why I said it, but now I had no way to rectify those words.

My father passed away from an inoperable brain tumor at the age of forty-two. I have recently just passed the day that officially saw me outlive him, a moment that hit me harder than I would have ever thought possible. His death had been expected, but it had never really sunk in that it would ever happen. I admired my dad more than anyone in the world and now see how his lessons and examples have stuck with me to this day, sometimes to a fault. My father was a smart, sweet, kind, social man who trusted everyone until they gave him a reason not to, and even then, he continued to give them a chance. It was just his nature. He had a temper that you did not want to be on the receiving end of, but it was usually called for when exposed. He came from humble beginnings, growing up on a farm in Avonton, Ontario, a small hamlet between Sebringville, Stratford, and St. Mary's, in a home that his grandfather had built and in which his mother was born. Typical of the times, my grandfather put the entire family to work once they were of age to fulfill farm duties. The work was hard and sometimes unforgivable—my grandmother even lost part of a finger—but they all participated for the betterment of the family.

My grandfather was business-minded, supporting his family off the land; later in life, he rented the fields to other farmers to supplement his income and maintain the land around his home during retirement. He lived a long life, passing in his nineties, and he was savvy enough to leave his children a little something after paying for a retirement home to live in after my grandmother passed. I could go on all day about my grandmother. She was lively, full of fun and had a cackle none of us will ever forget; I miss her greatly. It was hard work, but they did what was needed to feed the family, and they knew nothing else.

Later in life, my father worked as a maintenance man at a factory in Stratford. He wanted a family, and that desire overrode any financial or business aspirations he may have had. As with many people, his occupational title did not define him. My grandmother kept an old math exam of my father's from high school. He scored 105 percent on the test because there had been a bonus question. He was community-oriented, and he took pride in his home and neighbourhood. He volunteered at the community centre in Sebringville, helping with Scarecrow Day, the village clean-up day, and chalking the lines for softball and slow-pitch games. I remember going with him and watching him chalk lines. A little rickety container on two wheels poured the chalk as he attempted to walk in the straightest line he could down the first and third baselines. At home, he maintained the pool we had in our backyard, caring for the landscaping and pool house, and he erected the fence around the pool.

He worked shifts at a factory, and helped family and friends whenever a need arose, often after a protest from my mother. As one story goes, my parents were in bed sleeping in the wee hours of the morning when someone came knocking at their front door. My father popped out of bed, greeted the man warmly, only to discover that this young man had been extremely over-served at the local hotel. After a quick conversation, my father concluded that the young man was a long way from home and had no options, but Dad trusted he was a good person who was just in a bad spot. Dad got dressed and offered the man a ride to his home in Seaforth, ON, about an hour's drive each way. My mother, although rightfully angry, knew that this was the person she married; it was just his nature to be as helpful and kind as possible.

Many more examples follow a similar storyline. My favourite one was told as we stood in the receiving line at Dad's visitation prior to his funeral. An older lady told my mom a story that would seem unbelievable if you didn't know my father. We had a snowmobile for recreation, but often my dad would drive to work with it, usually on days when he wasn't sure his van could make it; he didn't want to miss a day's work if he had a way to get to the factory. On his way back home after work, he noticed a woman stuck in her driveway, trying to get on the road to drive in the storm he was trying to escape. Dad stopped to speak with her and learned she was trying to get to the hospital because her husband had just been admitted. He told her to stay there and that he would be right back. He drove home, gathered an additional helmet and snowsuit, and went back to get her and take her to the hospital. Again, he typically put others first, no matter how much it inconvenienced him.

My father was my hero, in how I saw him and in how I remember him. He is also my biggest fear: I am afraid of tarnishing the great name he built in forty-two short years through his actions, attitude, and zest for life and helping others, and I am afraid of disappointing him.

As I was growing up, Dad often said, "Jeff, never sell your name." Being young and easily distracted, however, this maxim never really set in. As I matured and gained life experience, the real meaning and weight of that phrase became more important. Whether it's five dollars someone lent you, someone needing a ride, or someone just needing a friend, all of your actions add up to what your name is worth to another person. If you think they have forgotten about the small bit of money you borrowed, whether they have or not, have you just sold your name for five dollars? If that person seeking a ride really needs to be somewhere, have you just sold your name for an hour of driving? Have you ignored the person seeking a friend? Have you just sold your name to avoid an awkward situation? I have deliberately carried this philosophy through life and into business.

About five months after splitting from my business partner in the orthotic industry, I followed the advice of smarter and more successful business people from whom I often would seek mentorship, and I started to diversify my portfolio. In June of 2018, I convinced my wife to make an offer to purchase some land by our home, despite her protests. The offer was accepted, and my wife and I were to take possession the following month. It was a double lot in the Old East Village of London, Ontario. Along with the property we purchased, the city approved architectural drawings and permits to build a brand-new fourplex. At this time, real estate was booming in London with high rental fees and low vacancies. I followed the advice of people I trusted to assess the land, get the sale done, estimate the costs accurately, and get the project started.

However, unbeknownst to me, my ex-business partner planned on violating our separation agreement and ceased using the services that he had agreed to as payment of my share value, effectively trying to steal that value from me. Based on the volume of business I was receiving from his clinics and the duration of the agreement, I should have had more than enough cash flow to complete this project in a timely manner and provide for my family, at the same time as I was growing my business. I had made large inventory orders to maximize discounts on my end, for which I was committed to paying since they had been received by my staff and inventoried for sale. We set up an e-commerce site, invested in developing new manufacturing milling machines, and started a marketing campaign.

I then received a letter from The Canada Revenue Agency (CRA) stating that my business, which I now owned one-hundred percent, owed Harmonized Sales Tax (HST) from the last four years, totaling eighty-nine thousand dollars in back tax with an additional twenty-five thousand in HST on the sales of that quarter's earnings of the fiscal year. Although the HST had been collected, it had not been remitted to the government. Additionally, I was looking at a number of expenses: recent orders that totaled over one hundred thousand dollars in inventory that would come due over the next three to six months, a construction project that would be funded by draws which reimburse expenses without advance payments to get ahead; a daughter who was about to have her first birthday, another daughter who was three years and eight months old, and the first luxury item I ever purchased for myself—a new car that I intended to pay for in cash. A few months prior to these revelations, I had been projected to earn over three hundred thousand dollars in profits that year, with approximately one hundred and twenty-five thousand owed to me in shareholder loans, but I now found myself struggling to pay my bills, knowing the cash would run out soon.

Things were very bleak; I had never been so low in my life. I felt like such a disappointment to the people who I loved the most and who relied upon me to provide for and protect them. I found myself in the darkest place I have ever been, surrounded by the darkest thoughts that I have ever entertained. Worse and worse news kept coming in the form of invoices for expenses, some expected and some unexpected. These needed to be paid to keep my doors open and to continue securing other investments and projects, which I was trying to complete to move the business exponentially forward, as I had intended to do as soon as I was legally separated from my old business partner.

Some people with whom I spoke about this situation told me to claim corporate bankruptcy and start fresh, but the thought of not paying other businesses for products or services that they had provided didn't sit right with me. I lost a lot of sleep most nights, which had never previously been a problem for me. My office building and my family home were security on the construction loan for the fourplex project, which was four months behind and over budget, in order to get the loan. I borrowed one hundred thousand dollars from my friend to pay my personal taxes, a by-product that I hadn't expected from the business separation. I owed contractors over two hundred thousand dollars; I owed one hundred fifteen thousand dollars in HST, one hundred twenty thousand in vendor debt, and my business running cost was over twenty thousand dollars a month. I hadn't received a paycheque in seven months; had a personal mortgage, car payment, and monthly expenses to cover; and I needed to help my wife provide for our family. The stress kept mounting on me, on my wife, on my children, on my life.

One night, after putting my kids to bed and sitting in my basement alone, I felt desperate and completely overwhelmed. I contemplated, "Should I just climb behind the wheel of that new, luxury car and never return?" I was aghast, nauseated by my own thoughts, but I felt trapped in a hole that I couldn't get out of without hurting my family. The situation seemed inescapable. I shook it off that night, but night after night, these thoughts crept into my mind. They were relentless, insidious, and, worst of all, part of my brain was making frantic calculations. Was a fatal accident the only viable solution? The thought of getting behind the wheel of my car and never coming back started to make more and more sense as the only viable solution. How could I get out, sparing my family from any more risk and protecting their future? The rationalization continued, slowly convincing me to take this final step.

"Your wife and children will be taken care of by the investments."

"You have over five million dollars to protect them in the event of death."

"Your debts would be paid."

"They are more important than you."

Not returning would have been a calculated move, galvanized by desperation. I gave this some serious thought and was nearly convinced that it was the only way to provide for my family. I paced around the kitchen, tears streaking my face. When your better angels are battling with the demons of despair, anger, resentment, depression, and you are overpowered by fear and disappointment, the idea of accepting a horrible choice is certain to arrive. I had accepted that this was it; this was the night. I had already experienced every stage of loss: denial, anger, fear, resignation, grief, and acceptance. I denied it was my fault; I was angry this had happened to me; I tried to negotiate with myself how to get out of it; I became depressed, and I finally accepted this was the only way—not as someone facing their end, but someone providing a future for his family. Again, I had never before considered death as an option, and in fact, I have always been horrified by it; nonetheless, I was prepared to go for my last drive.

But, instead of getting into my car and imagining how it would end, a different image arrived: my father's, which was followed with a new voice, a different voice, a voice not of disappointment, but warm with compassion.

"Never sell your name."
"Never sell your name,"

was the familiar refrain. I remembered what it was like without him for my mom, my siblings, for myself, and the emotional scars that remain today because of that loss. Although my death would be labelled as an "accident", the people closest to me, especially my wife's and children's pain, would be real and would stick with them permanently. Was I willing to sell my name as a coward, as someone that ran from his problems, for any amount of money?

No, I wasn't. A man's reputation is priceless. In the words of Guy Garvey, "Go straight to the place where you first lost your balance, and find your feet with the people that you love." I swallowed my pride and made a tear-filled call to my mother to ask for any help she could give. I am a proud, independent person, so even with my mother on the other end of the line, this call was extremely difficult to make. I broke down, trying to explain what had happened and saying that without her help, because I had nowhere else to turn, bankruptcy would be the result. The way I pleaded, the tone, and emotion in my voice alerted her mother's intuition to my shattered mental state, and she broke as well. The pain when one of your children is hurting doesn't stop because that child is an adult.

My mother has lost more in her lifetime and shared more heartache and pain than anyone should. She is strong, and although a bit cynical at times, not nearly as much as most people would be after everything she has experienced. She was the second oldest of ten children, and people relied upon her and expected her to do more than just an older sister normally did. As she always did for all her children, siblings, and father over the years, she and my stepfather offered me as much as they could, which afforded me three months of time. They continued to help with more financial aid where they could long after that, which gave me yet more time. I requested my cash surrender on one life insurance policy, which extended me another five months and kept vendors from sending me to collections. I cut staff hours; I moved my manufacturing to a cheaper location; and I changed our plans to reduce cost and altered our business model in hopes of increasing revenue. Even if I had to close my business, coming out of it with nothing, I had decided that I would do so without owing anyone any money.

To help pay the bills at home, I signed up to drive for Uber. I woke up between five-thirty and six in the morning and drove until the girls were ready to go to school and daycare. I drove them to their destination in my wife's truck, where their car seats were fixtures, and would get back home before my wife needed to leave for work. I would then drive for another hour before heading into work myself. Every opportunity I had, I drove through the day, provided it didn't interfere with the tasks needed to move my business forward. My wife would pick the girls up after work, and we spent quality time together as a busy family in the evenings. Once everyone was asleep, I went back out and drove until nine or ten at night or later, depending on the volume. Then I went home to sleep and repeat. On weekends, my wife would wake up with the girls and take care of them until I got back from the morning rides. I would spend some time with them, playing, cuddling, or watching television to calm them down a bit, put them down for their naps, and go back out and drive until they woke up. I would come home when they awakened and spend as much time with them or help a bit around the house. I'd get a short rest from the mid-afternoon until they were in bed for the night.

This schedule helped ease the financial burden slightly. But at times, I couldn't get out as much as I hoped due to obstacles my business or the construction project laid before us. I was embarrassed about having to drive for Uber to live and support my business and family, but I wasn't ashamed. The pace was relentless, but in the end, I did what I could while I could.

Most importantly, I didn't sell my name.

INTRODUCTION

What you're about to read is both a memoir and a manual of my experiences as an entrepreneur. It is intended to help you avoid the mistakes I made in business—mistakes that took their toll, financially and emotionally. This book is also a testament to how honesty and hard work, as well as staying true to my values and the humanity of others, allowed me to climb. As I write this, I am continuing my journey upward, with aspirations to surpass my previous successes.

Prior to their launch, many businesses will start with a *soft open*. Friends, family, and supporters of the entrepreneurs are invited to experience the product or service. Their feedback helps the entrepreneur(s) catch errors prior to the grand opening, which is, logically, called the *hard open*.

The term *hard open* has two definitions. It can mean an occasion *when* a business is opened to the public for the first time, not just to a limited number of people. However, another definition of a hard open is when a skydiver suffers an injury, sometimes fatally, because their parachute opens improperly or too quickly, usually a result of poor preparation. In this book, I illustrate how I dove head-first out of the plane and into the business world without the knowledge or experience to avoid a *hard open*.

Throughout this book, I will highlight the importance of each step of entrepreneurship, why you need to commit to each, and the negative impacts that can occur if you don't. This will illustrate how even decisions that may seem miniscule and unimportant when starting can undo everything you've worked for and sacrificed to achieve. I demonstrate this by detailing the errors I made and the repercussions that followed, including the stress and emotional cost to me and my loved ones. I will also share the steps I should have taken when I started in business and when I ventured into new projects. I will present a template that gives anyone the tools and playbook they need to protect themselves when they join the world of entrepreneurs. This book will teach you how to pack your parachute properly.

Business has always intrigued me. I believe that business can be extremely rewarding for people willing to take risks. I believe in innovation, I believe in the free market, I believe in one's ambition to overcome obstacles, I believe in being rewarded for hard work, and, most of all, I believe that you can be a successful businessperson without being unethical. I believe you can live the life you want and achieve your goals, and I believe you can do this without selling your name.

CHAPTER 1

THE ADDICTION

B eing an entrepreneur can cause you to behave as if you have an addiction. The word *addiction* is derived from a Latin term for *enslaved by* or *bound to*. Anyone who has struggled to overcome an addiction—or has tried to help someone else to do so—understands exactly why the description of being bound to or enslaved is suitable. Addiction exerts a long and powerful influence on the brain that manifests in three distinct ways: craving for the object of addiction, loss of control over its use, and continuing involvement with it, despite adverse consequences. Addiction affects the brain in a very specific way:

> The brain registers all pleasures in the same way, whether they originate with a psychoactive drug, a monetary reward, a sexual encounter, or a satisfying meal because pleasure has a distinct signature: the release of the neurotransmitter, dopamine, in the nucleus accumbens, a cluster of nerve cells lying underneath the cerebral cortex. Dopamine release in the nucleus accumbens is so consistently tied with pleasure that neuroscientists refer to the region as the brain's pleasure centre. An addiction of choice provides a shortcut to the brain's reward system by flooding the nucleus accumbens with dopamine. The hippocampus lays down memories of this rapid sense of satisfaction, and the amygdala creates a conditioned response to certain stimuli. Repeated exposure to an addictive substance or behaviour causes nerve cells in the nucleus accumbens and the prefrontal cortex (the area of the brain involved in planning and executing tasks) to

communicate in a way that couples *liking* something with *wanting* it, in turn driving us to pursue it. That is, this process motivates us to take action to seek out the source of pleasure. Over time, the brain adapts in a way that actually makes the sought-after substance or activity less pleasurable. *(Schaffer. Harvard Health Blog)*

If you have abused alcohol, drugs, or gambling, or if you know others who have, you will know that when they are just about to use or have just engaged in their addiction of choice, they will exhibit similarities to someone who is caught in the grip of an exciting idea. Similar to substance addictions, the brainstorming session becomes the agent of intoxication. However, the difference between entrepreneurial and other types of addictions is that entrepreneurial addicts always believe they have stumbled across something great. Also, similar to those we recognize as addicts, there is an obvious progression that the entrepreneurial addict follows:

1. The entrepreneur has had a breakthrough.
2. The entrepreneur maps out their idea.
3. The entrepreneur rationalizes the problem they will solve.
4. The entrepreneur produces the number of customers they will need or products they will sell.
5. The entrepreneur projects how much money they will make.

The excitement of researching the project, focusing on the fortune they foresee themselves accumulating, and the feeling that only they have uncovered this project is an entrepreneur's addiction. Like a gambler who believes their system provides the best way to beat the odds, you workshop the idea while trying to think of every angle, so others will not be able to poke holes in this *"brilliant"* plan. You formulate it, mould it, and take it to people you feel will understand it best. But also, like an addict, you take it to people who will tell you what you want to hear and encourage you. This *"feeds the beast,"* making you believe you have the next great idea. But here is where the problem lies; your enablers, although unwittingly, usually don't understand what your idea is, but they want to be supportive. In turn, their encouraging feedback makes you believe you can't miss, so you move forward with your plan.

Being a serial entrepreneur isn't necessarily a bad thing. An effective serial entrepreneur can avoid pitfalls. Like a drug, alcohol, or gambling addiction, however, the addiction of chasing that feeling, the *dragon*, as they say, can have the same negative result on you, your family, your friends, and your finances that those other addictions have if you can't control yourself and look through a realistic lens.

First, you must understand that every idea you have will not be a success; in fact, more ideas won't work than will. Second, someone else has probably thought of the same idea, and their attempt failed, or they didn't act upon it. That doesn't necessarily mean that the idea was bad or that that person didn't follow through on it. There are many reasons why people give up on ideas, such as:

- They don't have the needed financial resources.
- They don't have the confidence, connections, or know how to start.
- They don't have the mindset of entrepreneurs.
- They don't have the commitment, resilience, and a realistic belief to pursue the process.
- It was simply a bad idea.

Getting stuck or not getting started causes one set of problems. Being highly motivated can cause others. So when that feeling strikes and you're on the high, do all the things you normally do. However, when you take your *brainchild* to others for feedback, actually take your idea to the most pessimistic people you know. These people will give you the worst-case scenario. While they are critiquing the project, hear them out; take notes; go back to the drawing board. In other words, fill all the holes they have exposed. Do this again, and again, and again, until you can sit with your greatest critics and answer all their questions and debate all their comments. At that point, find a harsher critic. Do the same with them, and repeat this process as many times as you need to until you can, with all confidence, say you have a great idea worth looking into further and pursuing. Remember, even if your idea is great and you've *filled the holes*, you now have to find a market to buy what you're selling. That is where the real genius lies for most successful business people.

The feeling you get when you think that you have stumbled onto something no one else has thought of is euphoric. A person with an entrepreneurial mindset has ideas constantly running through his or her mind. The entrepreneur sees something—an event, a promotion, a business—and needs to know how it works and believes they can innovate a better or new way, or at least improve it to be more profitable. The entrepreneur believes no one else has thought of this product or of this new way of doing something. If you are this entrepreneur, you feel on top of the world, intelligent, warm inside, a sense of pride, a sense of ingenuity, and a feeling that you are meant for this. If you're like me, your brain is always spinning with every experience and event you attend. Like drugs, alcohol, and gambling, being a serial entrepreneur can make you want more; for some, that translates into not thinking logically about it. Chasing dragons can become chasing demons.

I once heard that a successful entrepreneurial venture stems from a string of failures. The entrepreneurs who succeed learn from each failure and come back for more, better equipped each time to make fewer mistakes and generate greater success. Like all desires in life, there is use and misuse, and businesses are no different. So, you have to ask yourself, are you a serial entrepreneur with healthy boundaries or just an idea person? A fine line separates the two.

When I was in my late twenties and finishing university, I worked at a restaurant that was very busy during the school year, but business in that area of London slowed down over the summer. This was really counterproductive for me, since I had more hours to fill shifts and make money during that season. To make better use of my summers, I decided to combine my hockey experience—I had been a player and a power-skating instructor—with the knowledge I had gained as a recent kinesiology graduate to develop a program under the name Core Conditioning. I focused on players who were playing AAA minor hockey and who had a chance of moving forward to junior or university hockey.

The program was a four-month-long syllabus of summer conditioning that was designed specifically for hockey players. It would start in May and end the week before tryouts. Core Conditioning involved taxing the lower body, core region, and anaerobic systems to mimic the energy used while on the ice. After school four days a week, I met ten teenagers at the local YMCA. We warmed up, did strength and core training, then finished with different aerobic or anaerobic training. As the summer progressed and we got closer to on-ice training, we shifted some of our focus on plyometrics, balance, speed, and agility. In the summer months, we started with an on-ice session at nine in the morning, followed by snacks, and then shuttled to the gym for half-past ten in the morning. Then we went back to the arena for lunch, an hour break, and an afternoon ice session with a few drills and some fun. I charged fifteen dollars per gym session for ten kids, four days a week for May and June. I was making six hundred dollars a week, plus my part-time work in the restaurant, where, most days, I didn't start until three in the afternoon and worked just two hours.

In July and August, the ice sessions were an additional cost to the clients of twenty dollars for players who had already enrolled, and twenty-five dollars for new clients electing to join coming just for the on-ice training. They all left at the end of the training with a manual that covered diet, sleep, on-ice tips, and goal-setting topics that we had discussed throughout the summer. I made this program affordable to most players' families looking to further their hockey experience, at the same time learned the value of working smarter.

I had two great summers; the program had the potential to be turned into a thriving long-term business with additional younger kids' camps in the summer and more sessions for older-aged players. As well, potentially I could have set up an in-season program to keep players involved all year. However, my complacency, lack of structuring, and failure to work the business properly brought it to an end. Although I knew active NHL hockey players with big names in the area at the time and was doing something different than everyone else, I simply assumed that people would keep showing up summer after summer. I thought I had found my golden goose.

I justified my *laissez-faire* attitude by reasoning that I was on my way to becoming a professional, and this was only a means to an end. I was wrong. It could have been a great business that I could have run alongside my current profession as a Pedorthist. I would have had time to oversee the training and enough enrollment to hire kinesiology students who were playing hockey at a junior or university level while in school. This business had the potential to double the income I was making as a pedorthist during the first five years I worked.

Currently, Dwayne Blaise, a friend of mine I met playing senior AAA hockey in Tillsonburg, Ontario, is doing all the things I should have been doing from the start. He has had so much success that he is the power-skating coach of the Washington Capitals and has a very successful company named Total Package Hockey (TPH) that is involved with the London Knights Academy. He makes a handsome living, has stayed involved in hockey, and works at improving his programming constantly, all things I could have strived for. I learned from my errors and moved on, carrying those errors of being complacent and recognizing potential with me. If I hadn't learned from this experience, I would have repeated those errors. However, I still remember the feeling I got when I decided to move forward with the program and initially contacted the original players to train with me; it was euphoric.

CHAPTER 2

ALWAYS BUYING SOMETHING

I have found that you cannot look at your business and expenditures only in terms of dollars and cents. No matter what decision you make, you are always buying something, and every action you take should be looked at as an investment. When business growth begins, especially with a small business, you constantly hit milestones that illustrate success, but these milestones also represent tipping points that have new expenses, require more investment, and necessitate new goals. As your revenue and volume increase, hopefully, so do your profits. At this point, however, you may need increased staff to maintain your service and free up some of your time, so you can maximize your skills and create more revenue. If you invest your time, be sure to get a return on that investment. Constant growth means more business, increased revenue, greater workload, and time spent fulfilling your business needs.

After leaving my position as a pedorthist for the first company I was employed by, I decided to join my ex-business partner to open pedorthic clinics in the Ottawa region. This meant a six-hour commute each way from London, the business had a higher cost in terms of my time than my money. This cost meant I could not spend time growing the two existing clinics in which I already had a strong presence and that were increasing in momentum. Every three weeks, I worked a full day on Monday in London, trying to fit in as many appointments as possible. Then, I left London and headed east on the 401 to Ottawa, getting there just before midnight, exhausted and ready for some sleep. Because I was there every three weeks, I had to do three weeks of work over three days. At first, this was not too bad. I saw three or four clients a day, assessing their conditions and dispensing orthotics, compression socks, and footwear. Then, I would drive the six hours back to London at the end of the third day. I usually stayed at my parents' home just outside Stratford and headed to Stratford Orthotics for nine the next morning to fulfil that week's appointments on Friday.

My time ended up becoming more valuable than I initially realized. I was unable to keep the southwestern Ontario clinics organized and appointment times full. Without being able to answer calls, respond to inquiries or emails, or follow up with clients properly, I left a negative impression with my clients at the two clinics that I had worked so hard to develop. This meant that I needed to trust someone to cover for me those three days, answering calls, setting up appointments, taking messages, and being the face of the company for old clients and the first impression for new clients. Additionally, this person needed to adhere to my mission statement and my principles for customer service as if I were doing the work myself. If policies can't be executed as they should be, the consequence of a neglected business will cost you far more than hiring an employee.

You might be able to find a person to work only three days a month who will do an adequate job, but that person will be very hard to find, and you will have to hire a part-time employee at the very least. Most likely, you'll need to hire a full-time employee to provide the service you want for your customers. For this person to meet my expectations, I had to meet theirs as an employer. This meant investing a fair amount of cash as we moved forward. However, to find someone you can trust to learn and understand exactly how the business should be run and to execute the business plan as you imagine it, you have to make that investment. This is true whether you're talking about a partner or an employee. in the result might be a godsend or a catastrophe, I experienced both.

Initially my parents, who were luckily both retired by this time and able to help, they oversaw my London and Stratford offices. Because of the time I spent traveling eventually I had to have someone, besides my parents, to maintain the offices. I found someone that today, almost a decade after she was hired, is still the backbone of my business.

I held interviews in Stratford to find someone whom I felt I could trust. I interviewed four candidates for the position, but two were simply too inexperienced to take on such a role. The other two both gave me a good feeling. One even had experience in a medical clinic; the other had recently sold her own business in another industry, and was looking for work. The candidate with the strong medical resume, however, had some specific requirements: a significantly higher wage than I was offering was the most pressing. I promised them both that there would be raises based on increased revenues, profit sharing, paid lunches, and eventually some sort of a health spending account. I stressed that the office would be a team environment. The medical clinic candidate said she'd get back to me. In the time she took to think about it, the other candidate was proactive and called me to follow up after the interview. My decision was made before that call was concluded. She wanted to grow with the company, felt she could contribute, and said she believed in my vision as I had explained it. She wanted to be a part of everything I mentioned I wanted to do. The new hire accepted my starting wage, was eager to learn about the industry, proved to have strengths that I lacked, and really helped push the business forward.

I invested in character and can say it was one of the best business decisions I have ever made. Today, she is making a good wage, gets profit sharing, takes time off when she pleases, and controls internal office matters. I have never been proven wrong to have invested such complete trust in her. She even brought her sister in to manage another location, and that decision has proven to be just as valuable. I constantly get positive feedback from clients about how great they both have been to interact with. Having two of them as staff, I have never had to worry in the office, which leaves time for me to focus on what I need to do to bring in more business or on ventures outside my main industry.

Meanwhile, I partnered with someone in Ottawa. To date, this was the worst business decision I've made, and I hope it always maintains that spot it's hard to believe anything could be worse. I met my ex-business partner through his cousin, who I worked with at a different orthotic business that I was contracted at in the Ottawa region. My ex-business partner was involved with that clinic as an interim contractor, getting additional shoe and other merchandise accounts for the manager and owner of that clinic. When his cousin explained to him in detail how their business model and promotions in the orthotic industry worked—and how luxurious the business model appeared to be on paper—he was intrigued to become a competitor.

Many clinics were giving similar promotions, so he was right to look into it and see if it would be viable for him. He quickly realized it could be, but he knew he couldn't do it on his own. He and his cousin started coming up with ideas and ways to make it work. They had vendor accounts, a pipeline to clients, and some experience in the industry. However, the biggest hurdle of this industry they had no solution to. Without a licensed clinician who had the proper accreditation, clients could not be reimbursed for their insurance claims. The two approached many professionals that were accredited, but none were willing to fill this role at an affordable price.

My ex-business partner's cousin approached me about coming on board. I said I would need to have a conversation with both of them together before deciding whether I could join the business. During our conversation, I got the feeling that my ex-business partner was a salesman. He laid out his resume through his business experience and offered to manage the administrative aspect of the business. With a small financial investment, I would be an owner and would be taking a big step toward meeting my goal of being self-employed in a viable business. This was the push I needed to commit fully and I did. However, red flags quickly began to appear, which I did not address as I should have.

I was now part of a business, I quit my job with the employer I had been working for, an employer who compensated me well, to engage in this business full time. I jumped into this partnership without even discussning a proper partnership agreement. I was excited about the Ottawa area and the possibility of this new business, and my ex-partner preyed on my inexperience and motivation to be self-employed. I partnered with this man who had been a salesman for most of his life, and he sold me on what he could do. He promised to run the business while I was in southwestern Ontario, so when I arrived every three weeks to assess our clients for orthotics and compression socks, the practice would run seamlessly.

At first, to his credit, he did attract business. He worked from noon through the rest of the day at the clinic, following his four-a.m. to noon shift at Home Depot. We were bringing in some revenue, and he inquired about quitting Home Depot to focus on the business. It made sense to have an invested member of the team trying to advance the business full time. Again, everything comes with a cost. Now he was receiving two thousand dollars a month while I worked for 'free' to keep money in the company as it grew. Five months after he quit Home Depot to be the company salesman and administrator, our business had only increased slightly. He also started delegating work to make his job easier. We were paying his cousin, his dad, and a full-time bookkeeper/receptionist to support him, I, the only clinician, was coming in every three weeks. The volume we were doing at the time was solid, but it was still in the infancy of potential I knew for that area. The two clinics I originally opened, prior to partnering with him, were almost at the same volume with one full time employee and myself managing. Within eight months of opening, the volume jumped significantly, but not enough to employ more staff, despite this, he hired another person to work full-time. So, at this point, we had six people doing the same work that three capable people should have been able to do. I protested, but not strongly enough, and I didn't demand anything.

I had my eyes set on another clinic in the area, thinking my partner could focus time there, shuffle some staff around to get it running and bring in the same volume without additional staff, to keep growing. I was wrong; he hired another person to run that location. We then discussed another location in Belleville, another area with a lot of potential. We found a space, signed a lease, and rented an apartment because we were spending more on hotel rooms than we would on this apartment. I learned later that he favoured the location and wanted an apartment there because his son had been recently drafted to the area's Ontario Hockey League team. This still seemed like a good fit, initially, as he would be in a good position to bring business in by meeting more people in the community. Later, I found out that in both Ottawa and Belleville, he was rarely at work.

A few years past and the profit didn't seem to reflect the revenue and volume of the three clinics we had together, and when I finally decided to sit with the accountant whom he had hired and go through the books, I thought it would take days to find the errors. I was wrong. Within twenty minutes of speaking to her about my concerns, she pointed out to me that he was putting his car lease, all meals at restaurants, gas, hotels (while off on personal recreational pursuits), and his family's cell phone costs all through the business. A few years later, he hired more employees than the volume of work could support; then completed a forty-thousand-dollar renovation on his home through the business and tried to hide it from me by including it in a renovation on one of our locations.

My partner had no intention of putting business first. It seemed that, in his mind, the money was his to do with as he pleased. Future business investments were not considered. Unfortunately for him, he filed for bankruptcy a little after we parted ways. The business lesson here is: if you want to show others how successful you are through showy materialism, you will deplete the resources that you need to really succeed. You will be unable to diversify investments, to increase your portfolio, to have long-term security, and to increase staff, product, or innovation. He invested in consumer goods and not in ways to further the business. A good entrepreneur practices delayed gratification until the time comes to safely and securely receive the personal spoils.

CHAPTER 3

DON'T PLAY CATCH-UP

If you want to create personal wealth or flourish as a business, you need to establish a plan with either a long-term or short-term strategy in mind, depending on your professional and personal goals. If you want to sell your business within five to seven years, it needs to show a strong profit for the greatest dollar value. If you want to run your business as your career, you will have a little more freedom on spending, but draining the account constantly will most likely end up causing you to shut your doors. Trying to impress people with success by increasing your debt with lavish material goods will eventually come back to haunt you.

When I was growing up, my mom was a teacher, before Ontario teachers received regular, steep pay increases, and when candidates took one year of teachers' college after high school to become qualified as a teacher. My father was a maintenance man at a local factory. They worked hard, and we didn't go without. I had three siblings who played competitive sports, and we had most of what other families had and everything we needed. But we didn't have expensive clothes, high-end cars, dinners out as a family, or many family vacations. The one family vacation we did have was a camping trek across Canada in 1986 to see the World's Fair in Vancouver, BC. We travelled in a van with a mini port-a-potty in it and pulled a tent trailer for our sleeping accommodations. I can still remember the smell of the KOAs we camped at and all the squeeze-play with which we entertained ourselves. Other than that, our vacations were mostly campgrounds within a distance of an hour or so from home. Looking back, I recognize how hard my mom worked—helping her father as he he aged; helping her siblings, as the second of ten children; managing her own family by making the smartest financial

decisions so she could clothe and feed four children; and dealing with financial troubles throughout her life. She truly amazes me. When I was in grade
six, I needed new indoor shoes for school. Most of my friends' parents had
higher-paying jobs or just indulged their kids, so those kids were wearing
the new Air Jordans or some hot trend of the time. My mom bought a pair
of Whiz Kidz running shoes for me, which she purchased at Bi-Way. They
served their purpose and fell in the price range she could afford. I was embarrassed and was made fun of a lot for wearing them, but they worked just fine,
and now have the utmost respect for my mother knowing her limits.

We all had summer jobs to support our social lives and then some, but
after my dad passed, things got really hard. I was an exceptional minor
hockey player, and at age fifteen, I started playing junior hockey. That meant
that instead of playing hockey with kids my own age, I was playing with and
against men as old as twenty-one. I am not a big man, and I was an even
smaller teenager. That season, I stood at five foot seven inches and weighed
in at one hundred and fifty-five pounds to start the season. My options to
try and advance my playing experience were either AAA in Waterloo, at a
significant cost to my mother, (which I believed she would have found a way
to pay for), or junior hockey, which was free, including some equipment. To
be honest, the thought of being around older guys and girls, going to parties,
and playing a higher level of hockey was very intriguing. The savings for
my mother's pocket book was on my mind, but as a selfish teenager, not at
the forefront.

Halfway through the year, I was offered the opportunity to finish the year
in Waterloo for the same team that had offered me a spot at the start of the
year. I had some injuries from playing against the much bigger and stronger
guys, and this looked like a great option to finish the year. After playing
against older guys, which improved my skills, speed, and level of confidence,
I thought I might be able to impress some scouts for a spot on a team the
following season at a higher level of junior. When I sat down with my mom,
after getting the call from the team in Waterloo, she said, without mincing
words, that we simply did not have the money for me to make this change. I
hadn't realized how much AAA hockey costs parents; not just in terms of team
costs but also the auxiliary costs for travel, equipment, and tournaments.

I stayed with the junior team. When the season was done, I was an Ontario Hockey Association all-Ontario champion, which led to a chance to participate at the under-seventeen tryout camp for Team Ontario with all the other players playing junior at the age of fifteen. I was also invited to play spring hockey with a team out of Durham, which would travel to tournaments all over Ontario in hopes of getting more exposure and attention of scouts. We found sponsors to pay some of the costs, but I had to go to the tournaments with friends and their fathers because my mom couldn't take time off work, and the cost of going to these tournaments was more than our family could afford at the time. I was lucky that a childhood friend was also on the team, and his dad was really understanding of my situation and helped us out with those things. I had a good experience and a lot of fun, but again, I was embarrassed because I had to sleep in other people's rooms and felt like a fifth wheel a lot of the time. No one did anything to make me feel that way, but I still felt like a charity case.

Later in life, while attending university, I was invited to play some beer league hockey and was lucky to become friends with some older guys, a few of whom were highly successful. I met one person through a mutual hockey acquaintance, who had ample free time and money, and we did a lot together. He was off work due to an injury, and I was in school. He paid for many of the memorable experiences I could have never afforded on my own, so I saw how the" *other half"* lived.

When I started making money and because I didn't have a family at the time, I narcissistically and stupidly thought I deserved to live the *good life*, especially because I grew up with financial restraints. I didn't blow all my money, but I also didn't save nearly as well as I could have. I was playing catch-up with the people close to me who were far more established. I leased a modest car, moved to a nice apartment, went out for dinner often, bought clothing, went on vacations more often. It felt good; I felt like I was a success. I thought I had earned it. What I came to realize was that no one cared but me. I didn't gain any friends or security by spending this way. I didn't have better memories, and I didn't impress anyone. I did put significant savings aside, relatively speaking, but I could have easily increased that amount.

Trying to make myself feel like a success caused me to spend a significant amount of money instead of making long-term plans. Most investments do not produce a substantial return overnight, or even over a decade, but they do require a substantial initial purchase. Playing catch-up to others is financial cancer.

Instead of mistakenly trying to improve the lifestyle I was living, I should have saved more money, made better investments, and planned for all situations right away, but I didn't. After a couple years, I did try to do just that; I moved into a smaller, cheaper apartment, drove the same car, and didn't spend too much money socially. Instead, I put all the extra money I made on my substantial student and business loans, which I paid off in two years of profitable work. After those debts were paid off, for the first time in my life, I had disposable money, and for the first two years after paying off my debts I saved a lot, but I realized that I spent much more than I should have. I was lucky enough to understand this in a couple of ways.

First, in year three of my business being profitable, I changed my spending habits slightly and made a loose, long-term plan, which turned out to be my saving grace. If I hadn't adopted this plan, my previous attitude would have cost me everything as it did my ex-business partner; I would have had to file for bankruptcy as he did. He got caught up in the same haze as a grown man with a family, as I had as a young single man. He never realized it and never changed his personal spending habits. This, unfortunately and ultimately, became a business problem because his habits increasingly affected the business cash flow and profitability. I remember getting a text from him once that said he wanted a boat, and he needed three thousand dollars more per month to afford the slip fees. He wanted to take that amount out as a dividend. As fifty-fifty business partners, legally, we both had to get the same amount in dividends. I reluctantly agreed, but I still agreed, which placed the stress of an additional six thousand dollars a month on the company. I sought out mentorship, and I followed the advice of my accountant and a couple of successful business associates. This is a great example where proper planning for a partnership can protect your business and you personally, which is discussed later in greater detail.

Second, I met my girlfriend, who is now my wife, and we started planning our life together. However, we never discussed in detail our personal wealth or spending habits. Most people try to avoid and dislike being called *cheap*, even if it applies to them. There is a fine line between cheap and frugal. An even finer line exists between those labels when they are applied to someone who is being smart with their money or who is being stupid with money and is being labelled cheap. To avoid being labelled cheap I made careless spending habits.

Being cheap carries a negative stigma, and it can certainly be negative. For example, if one is so cheap that people recognize tactics that are being used to avoid paying their fair share, it is definitely a negative. However, living within your means and simply not doing more than you can afford to do is smart. I have always said, "I work to live, not live to work," and I believe that. I feel bad for people who miss out on great life experiences for themselves and their family, just to look at their bank account and see a number. Usually, no matter how much is there, it is never enough for these worriers, and the idea of parting with their money for even the smallest thing makes them very anxious. Security is a good feeling, but as with everything, moderation is the key. Alternatively, trying to impress people by having an expensive car, big house, tickets to every event, expensive vacations, and buying drinks and dinners will only get you into debt and usually doesn't impress anyone. The people with money don't care—they could do that too, if they wanted to—and the people without money might see you as arrogant.

My wife isn't cheap; she occupies a *centre spot* that leans towards sensibleness. She will go on trips and out for dinner, but she also price-matches at grocery stores, looks for sales, shops on community websites, and looks for a discount wherever she can. I never really followed those kinds of practices because they always seemed like such small change in comparison to the hassle. In business I looked at everything as money, but personally, I didn't care. My wife made a plan for where her income would go, and she stuck to the plan as best she could. She has done so since she started working and it has paid off for her.

Instead of spending all your profits on personal wants and improving your lifestyle slightly as you make more money, you can use your profits in a more efficient manner to increase your business wealth, which, in turn, will increase your personal wealth. Hopefully, you will spend many years on this planet, which means you need to plan your finances to line up with that lifespan. If the longest journey starts with one step, don't make that journey harder by adding the weight of debt on your back.

CHAPTER 4

STARTING A BUSINESS

Starting a business is a nerve-racking, daunting, but extremely exciting experience.

Everyone will tell you to write a business plan. That is sound advice, so follow it. Ask yourself why you want to start a business. Writing down ideas leads to more ideas, which leads to more questions, which leads to more doubts, which will eventually lead to a conclusion. However, no one tells you what to do once you have a business plan completed. When starting a business plan, the product is your first concern, with the following provision: how much of your *product* is your business, and how much of your business is your product? This is an essential question that many businesses never fully understand the importance of finding the answer to, and that failure causes them to never meet their potential, or even worse, to fail.

In London, Ontario, there are some great supports for small business. You can take classes with the London Small Business Centre and other places, such as the Tech Alliance, none of which have a vested interest in your plan other than to provide constructive criticism as they go through your idea with you from start to finish. These options may have a minimal cost, if any, but are worth any cost that might be incurred. After experienced and objective eyes see and critique your plan, you may ask yourself again: will or won't this business work? Remember, a business plan gives you a map and helps you consider all the angles. If someone does not understand the plan, it does not necessarily mean that the business is a bad idea. Some of the greatest entrepreneurs were told multiple times their businesses would never work, so take the counsel of these experts, but don't ignore your gut feelings about your idea.

Ask yourself: Am I willing to fall on my face? Will I sacrifice just about everything to make my idea work, even during the worst of times? In my opinion, the biggest question you need to ask yourself and give an honest answer to is: what do I want out of it? Now, on the surface, your answer might seem easy, and it is if you provide the typical rhetorical answer, but honest, deeper answers provide a better road map as to what you want and how to get there.

When I finished my undergraduate studies at Western University in kinesiology, I was faced with the same question that every undergraduate faces: what am I going to do now? I didn't know. I was working in a restaurant, teaching at hockey schools, and doing some group training with young athletes. With a kinesiology degree, your options are limited if you don't want to move onto postgraduate work. I decided I needed to find a career, and that meant postgraduate studies, but in what? I wasn't sure how to narrow the scope down, and at this time, I was thinking more about healthcare than business. I asked a physiotherapist if I could shadow him for a little while and see what that was like. I spent a week at the Fowler-Kennedy clinic in London. They had me administer ultrasound treatments, help clients with exercises, and discuss injuries and possible treatments. They also advised me on the next steps a person in my position would have to take to get to their position. It was fast-paced; they saw a lot of people in a day. They seemed like they were always playing catch-up, but they were highly educated people who knew how to put the body back together.

I was intrigued but still not sure. I decided to shadow another professional, a chiropractor. Again, I went through their daily routine of seeing patients and observing them doing adjustments.. Chiropractors are also highly educated and well-trained professionals who help a lot of people. I found this profession to be a good fit—more my pace—and I was seriously considering applying to different chiropractic colleges. I found myself asking business related questions more often than practice related questions. The clinician asked me why I wanted to go into healthcare and specifically into chiropractic practice. My first answer was the automatic one, "I want to help others and have a respected career that my education supports." This mission might not be a bad answer to offer if in a job interview, but it was not the truth. He then challenged me to be honest about why, so I said, "I want to set my own hours, have room to grow, and make good money." He persisted, seeing that I was being a bit more sincere with my second answer. I replied, "I want to make really good money and enjoy my life." After getting that answer out of me, he told me not to go into chiropractics, but to look into pedorthics, so I did.

Pedorthics made a lot of sense for what I wanted to do. It could be lucrative, had retail and manufacturing components, was scalable, and eventually, I could have others working for me, rather than doing all of the appointments myself. The truth is that, at the time, I didn't really care if I helped people, nor did I care about being recognized as a highly educated person; I wanted to grow a business. I also understood that the best way to grow a business, especially a referral-based business, is to help people get the results they desire and to be genuine with those people. So to get what I wanted from clients, I had to help them get what they wanted from me.

Every person I see gets a full assessment that is often more thorough than previous examinations my clients have experienced with other practitioners in this field. Patients are educated on the conditions we see, on how those symptoms affect them, and how these factors can contribute to pain in all areas associated with that condition in their body if they are not addressed.

In healthcare, there can be a lot of arrogance rather than actual knowledge. On one hand, many clinicians believe they are the clinician and you are just the client; they know best, and you should do as they say. On the other hand, many clients self-diagnose, advise the clinician, and determine the results prior to professional advice. I have never endorsed either of these approaches. I learned, while working in restaurants, that you sell yourself as much as you sell your products. I talk to people as equals, give them honest feedback, educate them as to why they might be feeling the way that they do, describe how I can help, and I don't promise any outcomes. The only promise I make is that I guarantee my products and services and will warrant them for as long as the client has them. Trying to make money at every turn makes you seem shady and leaves people with the impression that you're more about their wallet than you are about them. So, for me, what I really wanted was to be successful on my terms, have the freedom to take chances in other ventures, and live a secure life but one marked by fun. If the chiropractor hadn't made me answer his question honestly, I might not have chosen this career path.I also want good results for my clients and that will contribute to my positive reputation and my business.

Whether you know exactly what you want to do or you fall into it, as I did, you need to have a strong, structured plan prior to opening your business. A finished business plan is much like a PhD dissertation. When candidates try to achieve a PhD, they invest themselves in their studies. They ask a question, theorize a solution, and research or experiment with the information and facts that they gather to compile a document in which they explain their work and their conclusions. They stand by their work and present it to a panel of experts who question them on each area of their dissertation. They know that their hypothesis could be incorrect, which would be disappointing, but contributes to the field of study and maintains the strong scientific process. The results confirm their next hypothesis, so too, with a business plan.

To be granted a PhD, the candidate must successfully defend all parts of their work with solid research and clearly illustrate their conclusions. You, as a competent entrepreneur, must be able to do the same. When being criticized or queried about your business plan, you must defend what you believe is the best solution to the problem at hand, which, in your case, is the best way to do business in that particular market. If you cannot defend all parts of your business plan, you're not ready to go to market or even seek investment, you need to go back to the drawing board. If someone inquires about an area of your plan that isn't clear, it may be that the plan isn't crystal clear to others although it is to you and you need to improve your articulation. You must be able to explain why the area has been designed and included in the way that it has been. If you cannot offer answers to questions that directly relate to your business plan, one of the following four things is going on:

1. **You have overlooked something pertinent and need to do more research to come up with a conclusion.**
2. **The point is a variable that you can explain, but you may not be able to articulate a precise answer.** If it's the latter, that's fine, provided you have a clear answer to what you expect to do in that case. Changes will occur as your plan goes from theory to practice, your answer may depend on what stage the business is in or entering. Your answer will depend on what your business can do at that time and what you've learned up to that point.

3. **The question or point of view is irrelevant, however, having someone ask the question will motivate you to explore before coming to that conclusion.** For example, I have finished a plan for an innovative business and social model that reduces costs and provides the best available services for families that are expecting a newborn. This business would support the different needs which will occur from the prenatal stage through the first year of a child's life. Because we have a socialized healthcare system, my plan depends on the province covering the cost of all the services. I have to be sure all avenues of this business plan can be defended. I considered medical care, social care, financial care, and politics, and I devised a plan that reduces costs by approximately twenty percent of current birthing costs; provides excellent healthcare; increases social supports for the clients; and is friendly to all political platforms. I believe I have achieved a complete plan and am ready to defend it, and I am trying to get the right people to present the plan to the provincial government, seeking approval to create a pilot project to demonstrate how effective the plan can be. I may not get approval, and this plan may never come to fruition, but I have covered every angle in the event that I get a chance to present it to Ontario's or other provincial governments.

4. **You have a bad plan.** Be prepared to scrap it.

When I started in this industry, I worked for a man who was money-driven and governed only by profits. He kept his costs as lean as possible, maximized profits, and did very well financially; however, he focused only on those two things, cost and profit. For instance, his locations, which I worked out of as a healthcare professional, were less than desirable, and he discouraged the extra work that I tried to add into services for the clients because he wanted short assessments that brought people in and out as fast as possible. When I went to work for myself, I took this lesson with me. My product was mainly orthotics, with footwear, compression socks, and braces as auxiliary products. I, along with every other person in my industry, offered the same products to help alleviate pain with one device or another. I account for our physical product as being only about fifty percent of what we offer. The remaining fifty percent that would complete what we want to provide, to complete our product, included:

- Personality
- Empathy
- Understanding
- Time
- Atmosphere
- Convenience

These provisions are crucial and deserve a more detailed discussion.

PERSONALITY

I refer to *personality* as just being able to talk freely with clients and to allow clients to ask questions and feel comfortable. I have mentioned before that creating this type of safe space is a skill and depends on your personality. There is an abundance of arrogance in the medical world, where clinicians work hard to become educated and stay up to date so they can offer the best knowledge possible. However, acting as if your opinion and your observations are the only legitimate advice and service available is not an enjoyable expierence, and patients may avoid you based on that impression. Speaking to them as equals and educating them about their issues has always allowed me to get my suggestions for treatment across effectively and allows clients to be a part of the solution. I cannot count how many clients I have had come in and say after an assessment, "The last person just did their thing and told me they would contact me when the orthotics were ready." They left those appointments not knowing why they were in pain in the first place, or how the decisions and designs could help them.

My method goes even further in terms of word of mouth. If people like you, they are inherently biased towards you and want to see you do well. Statistics show that doctors who end up being sued for malpractice are generally the ones that have a bad bedside manner (Gladwell 40-41) . Even if a practitioner's work is exceptional, a patient who is unhappy is more likely to sue or speak negatively of you in their circles and to other professionals, thus diminishing your referral base, if they don't like that healthcare professional. An unhappy person may never give you a second chance because of their negative opinion of you and your company, even if they do not go to the point of legal action.

Your personality and it's impact on a self-owned company, don't clock out at the end of the work day. I have made a lot of positive connections over the years with great people by simply trying to treat everyone with respect and dignity.

EMPATHY

Too little empathy and too much focus on only dollars and cents can make your customers feel like a product themselves and cause them to feel little connection to you as a person. Without empathy, people can interpret that you don't care about people and care only about their wallet. However, too much empathy can set you up for a different problem. Empathy without boundaries and limits is a difficult situation to recover from. Clients can test the limits of your empathy.

I once had a person I know come in after he had lost his job a few months earlier. He had also just got out of the hospital after being assaulted, and he was trying to get back to work. He had severe pain and was finding it tough to get through the day, a difficult situation for someone who was both figuratively and literally trying to get back on their feet. I offered to do a full assessment and make a custom pair of orthotics for him for free. I felt dreadful. Sure, he had always been good to me and, at that moment, money didn't matter as much as getting him back in a position where he could become employed and back on his feet. He loved watches, and over the years, he had assembled quite a nice collection of them. On a day when I wasn't in the clinic, he dropped one off to my manager for me as a thank you. I was flattered and a bit embarrassed when I received the unexpected gift. He not only brought that gift but also referred other business in our direction. This man was obviously one of the clients who respects kind gestures and felt appreciated; however, others will take advantage.

I have sponsored so many magazine ads for fallen soldiers, the OPP, The Canadian Legion, and many others who have asked. I received little business, if any, from a number of these groups, but because I see them as providers of good services and people with good intentions, I have wanted to help where I could. I have a soft spot for veterans, the elderly, and first responders. However, I believe donations should be reflected in your business success, so if you have no business and a lack of funds, you should not make such donations or subsidize individuals. Being smart and business conscious does not make you a bad or selfish person, and having empathy may not mean that you can or should always underwrite the cost of services, especially when it is not financially feasible.

UNDERSTANDING

Understanding is different than empathy. To be understanding is more about being open-minded and rational about issues other than your own. Things can happen unexpectedly to people and yet the world doesn't slow down. I have no problem listening to others when they explain their issues to me, and I can be empathetic. With understanding, you may connect with another person's issue and help with a solution, but at the end of the day, your business cannot be a charity.

For example, in healthcare, someone may need care but can't afford to pay for it all up-front, or their benefits may not have kicked in to cover their healthcare related expenses. I once had a client who came to see me because he had a severe case of plantar fasciitis, which can be very painful. This person came in after he had started a new job that had him on his feet for most of the day in safety shoes. He hadn't worked in a few months and was wearing his old safety shoes, which had seen better days and were a major contributor to his issues. Unfortunately, his job was causing him extreme pain, which forced him to take a day off, and he was worried that he would lose his job if he needed to take any more days off. But he couldn't get rid of the pain without more rest and time off of his feet to recover. Additionally, he had to work for three months before receiving benefit entitlements, and he was only in week five.

After the assessment, he was happy to know that his condition would clear up relatively quickly and that he would be able to work pain free with a new pair of boots and custom orthotics. The problem revolved around the fact that he had been off work for a long time before securing this job, and he was short on cash and without benefits for seven more weeks. We had to find a solution. I felt bad, but if I sent someone away with free orthotics and advice every time a similar situation arose, I would be devaluing my profession, education, and business. The other possible issue was that others from his place of employment might possibly expect the same treatment for the same cost if they were to come in. So, I proposed a solution. I told him that we would modify his safety shoes for fifty dollars, which usually would cost one hundred dollars. That would help ease the pain in his feet until the new benefit plan took effect. If he came back for a follow-up assessment when he had benefits, we would use the fifty dollars as a deposit toward his custom orthotics, which would cost four hundred dollars at time of pick-up. He agreed. We modified the safety shoes, and he was able to work in relative comfort for the next eight weeks until he received his benefits.

He came back in for the follow-up assessment to be sure we hadn't missed anything and nothing new was presenting itself. He was thankful and fully recovered within a couple weeks of receiving his custom orthotics. He has been a consistent customer and advocate of our services since. A little under-standing went a long way.

TIME

Every business has a different model, even those in the same industry. In my experience working in auto shops, construction, landscaping, retail, res-taurants, gyms, hockey schools, and now healthcare, people feel appreciated and cared for when you give them an appropriate amount of *time* to explain themselves and make time to answer their questions and educate them on their needs.

In my industry, I once worked at a place that was far more concerned about getting as many people as possible through the doors and up-selling every product they could to maximize revenue. This isn't a bad business prac-tice if it is done with integrity. When working at this place, the boss, who was not a clinician, sat me down and told me that he thought I needed to resolve a couple issues that had caused others some grief. I was surprised, but if I could improve my performance, I was willing to do so for the betterment of the company.

First, I was told to shorten my assessments, so we could fill more appoint-ments per day. While working for this employer, I was travelling from London to Ottawa, Orillia, Kingston, and Sarnia, which meant that I was only in Ottawa six to nine days a month and the others four to six times, depend-ing on the time of year. Limited days at each clinic meant more volume on those days to equal the volume of a full months schedule. I would take up to forty minutes for a complex assessment, but I averaged around twenty-five minutes per assessment; however, my employer wanted me to cut them down to fifteen minutes. Basically, I was there for minimal clinical work and to sign for those claims that were covered by the client's insurance company. Second, I was told to keep the orthotic as basic as possible because some of my designs were causing the manufacturers to have to put more effort than usual into making them, and the additional complexity was slowing them down.

This business model focused on revenue, not client care. The business did well and made a lot of money, but it became known more for the deals people could get there than for the actual positive results regarding healthcare. Since working for myself, I have had many occasions when I have spent an hour or more with clients with most of the clinical work being completed in twenty-five to thirty minutes. I have even had my office manager come in and interrupt an assessment because someone else had arrived. For many clients, a sympathetic ear is what they want and need at that moment. We have all heard the phrase time is money, but referrals and word-of-mouth advertising are money, and these people are usually the best source of both.

ATMOSPHERE

Atmosphere is another variable in business and in business models. For me, the atmosphere isn't just the furniture and art on the wall; it includes everything that affects the work environment, from the way we answer the phone to the way we say goodbye. I have great staff that attempt to make the entire experience as pleasant as possible, but who also add to our office's atmosphere by going above and beyond my expectations.

When someone calls to inquire about our business or finds us through an online search, our atmosphere starts right then. Do prospective clients get a warm feeling when we greet them on the phone? Do they feel they are appreciated and served the best we can during time on the phone and right after the call? When they arrive, are they met with a smile and someone who is willing to listen to them, no matter how busy we are? Is our business clean, organized, and welcoming for someone who has to wait until their appointment starts? Is the temperature at a comfortable level, no matter the season or what is happening outside? Is the furniture new(ish) and stain free, and is the office void of clutter? Is there complimentary water, tea, or coffee for them? Do they know where all the amenities are in the building? Does everyone operate within their scope of knowledge, so clients know that they are getting the best information we can possibly give them? When they leave each representative of the company, do they feel good about bringing us their business? Will they leave feeling they would put their name out there and send us referrals? All of this adds to the atmosphere of your business.

CONVENIENCE

As real estate people say: location, location, location. However, a great location is just the start, *convenience* is often more important. Some businesses are very specific, and location doesn't always matter. But for anyone with stiff competition in their field, location can be a make-or-break situation.

People are becoming more efficient and feel that they don't have time to waste. Picking a location is extremely important, often for reasons many do not consider. A location must check the boxes for its particular city or town: transit system, traffic flow, and, possibly the most important factor, parking. First, are you in a big city, small city, or a town? Larger cities, especially if you chose to be right downtown, don't always require parking, and if it is required, the citizens are used to paying for it. Many people in larger cities take subways, buses, ubers, or taxis. Some clients may require paratransit, which has a higher standard for safe travel than regular transit. Are you close to any of those options, meaning, is a subway platform or bus stop close? Can an uber or taxi easily pick up and drop off people? In smaller cities and towns, most people drive and don't like to pay for parking, so is there a free lot on-site? These considerations are big factors that you need to consider before buying a building or signing a lease. Depending on the type of business, such as retail, where people may be leaving with multiple items, many don't want to have to carry those items far to stow them away until they are ready to head home.

In cities of all sizes and in some towns, there are restricted-turn lanes. You may have a great location in the city that is close to a number of other amenities, but the corner or street you're stationed at can only be accessed from one direction, on one part of the street. This doesn't seem like much, but someone who hates dealing with traffic may go somewhere else because of it. Additionally, are there any city infrastructure plans that could alter the street that you are about to be located on for the next number of years? You frequently see instances where a retail or restaurant space has changed hands three, four, five or even more times. The new owners change some design elements and the colours and try again. They see a busy corner or street where their business should thrive, and yet none do. People want convenience, and, if only at a subconscious level, these things can be the difference between a successful business or having your location empty and failing.

In short, your product is everything attached to you as a business and possibly more. If you're in a competitive business and you are qualified to serve your product, what makes your product better than that of the person beside you?

Humans inevitably buy into *sensation transfers*. In his book *Blink*, Malcolm Gladwell describes sensation transfers as occurring when people favour a brand or product due to the surrounding input they unconsciously receive. The unconscious will steer the customer to choose what they like most without them knowing it. These sensations include anything from the first impression, to advertising, greeting, packaging, service, and the product itself. He further describes the Pepsi Taste Challenge in the nineteen-nineties. When tasters were asked, after a sip of cola, which cola they preferred, most tasters preferred Pepsi over Coke. This response alarmed Coke, which led to a change in the recipe and further led to a return to the original recipe, now branded as Coke Classic. The reason the tasters choose Pepsi over Coke is that Pepsi was sweeter than Coke, so with only one sip, the reaction was more favourable to Pepsi. However, when researchers did not rely on only one sip and they displayed the brand, the tasters' unconscious picked up all the information it deemed pertinent to their decision, even subtle clues. Colour, packaging, shape, and even the size of the can will all set a preconceived notion of what that person prefers (Gladwell, 160-166).

Big brands have the advantage in that they can advertise for the lifetime of clients, but as a small business, you, for the most part, do not. If you want to use the effective measures of sensation transfers, you need to provide a smooth, uncomplicated, and gratifying experience every time someone enters your business. I believe that if you strive to provide upper-echelon service, products, and the items I have listed, and you are willing to continually evaluate where you can improve, you will offer a product that is better than most of your competition. Your product itself may not be any better than your competitors, but by providing the greatest complete package possible, you will play on clients' sensation transfer, forcing them to favour your business.

CHAPTER 5

PLANNING SUCCESS

Business, in the end, is about results and creating profits to lead to personal wealth. Like planning what you will do to build your business, you also need to plan personal wealth management in the most efficient way. This planning will provide financial security and increase your portfolio at a much faster rate than if you do not plan. There are a number of issues that need to be considered to achieve this success. Whether or not you execute any or all of these actions, you should know what is available to you as a business person:

ACQUIRE A MENTOR

A mentor can be someone in your family, a friend, or hired personnel if necessary. If possible, find more than one; perspective comes in many forms, as do solutions to problems. Ideas, plans, roadblocks, and issues may require different skills to navigate, and the more people with varying skills you can turn to, the less your burden and stress when finding a solution. When we have an issue as children, we go to the people we think will have all the answers: our parents. If our parents are not available, we approach grandparents, aunts, uncles, or other trusted adults. We go to them believing that they have all the answers because they are older, have more experience, and we know they have our best interests in mind. So find a mentor you can trust to have a mentality similar to that of a parent. If you know there is no ulterior motive, you can take their advice at face value. There are professional services that offer business coaching and online courses that can be helpful. But beware: these people are out for profit and not for your gain, and they have no vested interest in your business or success.

BUSINESS PLAN

A business plan lays out what, how, when, where, and why you want to open a business in a particular market. If you have a great business plan and can defend it so strongly that it makes sense to pursue the business, you now have to plan for a successful business.

First ask yourself these questions: will your business be a solo venture or will you take on a business partner? What are your goals and objectives? What is your product? When wealth starts to accumulate, what will you do with it? Do you plan to sell within a certain period of time or keep the business until you retire? Do you plan to have multiple streams of income or other investments? Do you plan to be *hands-on* from day one, or are you planning eventually to oversee the operation instead? What's your mission statement? What are the competitors doing? How does your SWOT (Strength, Weaknesses, Opportunities, Threats) analysis look? An honest approach will reflect your strengths; play to these. Potential clientele will recognize your strengths immediately.

Further, be aware of your weaknesses and improve on them constantly. Eliminating as many weaknesses as possible will only add to your list of strengths. Make the most of your opportunities, recognize them, keep to your plan to realize them, but constantly review your progress, so you do not limit other potential opportunities to expand your business. Understand and be fearful of threats to your business. They are real; they can sink you, and new threats will develop throughout different stages of your development and expansion.

Where do you fall in your PEST (Political, Environmental, Social, Technological) analysis? Political positions, in business, do not always, but may, reflect your personal political views. Ask yourself whether political policies will benefit or impede your business. Many companies that have achieved billions in assets and values have done so because of one political policy that went in their favour; if this policy had not had a favourable outcome, it could have devastated their business.

Environmental issues, even if they fall within the letter of the law, can give your brand a bad reputation, depending on other factors in the business plan. For example, if you open a coffee shop with the hopes of expansion and franchising, where, how, and from whom you get your beans, cups, and lids, and how you dispose of them can be a strength to attract customers or can be the demise of your entire plan.

Social contributions, again, depend on your industry. Do you need to engage in the community to attract customers? If so, a plan that describes in detail and a budget for how these contributions will be executed must be reflected in your business plan.

All companies need some form of technology. Will your business need high-tech, modern technology? Who will maintain it? How much is the initial cost? How much are the maintenance costs? Will technology change? If so, on what time frame?

The PEST analysis, like most of your business plan, may raise more questions that need to be answered before you move forward. Once all these questions are answered, you may already know, but want to ask again: who are your customers? Where will you locate? Will you expand, and if so, in what time frame? What are your costs? What are your projected profits?

FIND PROFESSIONAL SERVICES

At the start, get a business lawyer and a good accountant. I currently have excellent resources in both areas, but that was not always the case. When I decided to go into business with my ex-partner, I trusted that we were both shooting for the moon and would both do anything to get there, so I went against the advice of others and did not consult a lawyer who represented my interests.

A lawyer, even in a partnership arrangement, analyzes all agreements and opportunities, protecting their client's interests. When we started the business, my partner and I had no formal partnership agreement; he convinced me that the shareholder agreement in the minute-book constituted a partnership agreement, something a lawyer seeking my best interests would have explained did not during consultation, had I sought a lawyer's advice. Because we did not have a partnership agreement, it was legally impossible for me to change anything, which ultimately led to the demise of the partnership and to the financial struggles we both endured.

Had I consulted a lawyer and described what I wanted, I would have been advised to get these few key clauses and arrangements in the agreement:

1. **Decision making:** Are you equally involved in all decisions? If not, what/who is authorized for what role/decision?

2. **Sale of the business:** If you get an offer to purchase the business and only one party wants to accept the offer, who and how will you decide?

3. **Shotgun:** If there is a breakdown in the relationship, is there a way for the parties to part ways? The shotgun ensures that you can establish a floor for the price of the shares if you want.

4. **Death/Disability/Divorce/Bankruptcy:** If one of these triggering events happens to one party, what rights does the other party have? Any one of these things could destroy a business. A proper agreement will protect the other party from disaster if one of these unfortunate issues arise.

5. **Non-competition:** If one party ceases to be a shareholder, can the departing shareholder start a new competing business? If so, should the departing shareholder be allowed to freely solicit or interfere with any suppliers or customers of the business?

6. These are only a few considerations, but a lawyer can advise you on every aspect of your business.

7. The second key service is provided by an accountant. A good accountant will help you organize your books and taxes, and advise you on cash flow and projections for your fiscal year. They will properly file sales tax and your fiscal year ends with the government for you. They will also advise you on tax savings by structuring holding companies and dividends, amongst other strategies, to maximize personal wealth. An accountant who stays up-to-date with legal and governmental changes will also plan a sale for your business that maximizes your company value and reduces personal tax so you can walk away with the most cash in your pocket as possible.

DO YOUR HOMEWORK

This should be done as part of your due diligence when starting a business plan, but revisiting this portion of that plan and building on it in case something is missed is very important if you are going to stay up-to-date and see all potential threats.

I have already spoken of increasing your portfolio, which refers to venturing out into other industries or making investments outside of your own scope of business. If you chose to do that, doing your homework is even more important. It is smart to have multiple streams of income, but going after something new that is not already in place, that you don't thoroughly vet, can set you back years, or even break you. Even if you have a good handle on the venture you are thinking about undertaking, there can be many intricacies that will escape you unless you have been directly involved in that industry.

The same can be said about changes to your industry through regulations or shifting consumer trends. One example is insurance. It is legally necessary to own or lease a building to operate as a professional, and it is important to protect yourself in worst-case scenarios. However, do you know what insurance is best to get? How much coverage will you need? What will the premium cost? For example, a company that removes snow for residential and/or commercial properties can offer to salt or not salt the parking areas and walkways. If a snow removal company offers to salt those areas, which, as a business owner, you should always request if your weather conditions warrant it, accept the offer; then, if anyone slips and falls on the affected areas, the snow removal company is liable. In recent years, the insurance premiums for snow removal businesses have increased to the point that, unless they have mass volume, it is not profitable or worth the business's time. Someone who accepts contracts prior to investigating this liability may work for free that season, or worse, if it is tied to summer property management, have those clients expect the same winter service, at the same cost every year.

I referenced the fourplex experience earlier, and it supplies another example of rushing into something only knowing sixty percent of the total cost of a project. Before building the fourplex, I looked into land costs, estimated costs to build (adding twenty-five percent to the estimates), property taxes, rental rates in the area, and the future prospects of a sale in the area. The gains on the investment were strong, but when building actually began, a

37

few complications emerged that I hadn't thought of and/or did not get good advice about. On top of the estimated cost to build, property cost, and rental rates, were costs and issues I didn't anticipate, which had a very negative effect on the profitability of the project:

- Auxiliary costs such as washroom facilities, security fencing, and garbage collection
- Total bank, appraiser, mortgage broker, lawyer (lenders especially), utility company fees, and interest
- City security deposits
- Lender's process for construction lending
- Final appraisal process and how appraised value is determined

All these items became an issue with our finances as I went about paying contractors and determining our final costs and affordability. In reality, having a better handle on these costs and on expectations about getting the job done would have changed my minds about doing the project, or at the very least, could have changed the types of work and materials that I put into the build to minimize costs. You hope that the people you ask will tell you everything, but that isn't their job, nor is it their responsibility when creditors come calling.

If you don't venture out into new investments and stay strictly in your industry, these same issues will still arise, as you need to hire staff, issue raises, cover health benefits, formulate company policy, and increase purchase of inventory/materials. If you don't include all associated costs, you may pay much more than you expected.

In my orthotic business, at its peak, we had eighteen employees, revenues that totalled over four million dollars annually, and were still looking to grow. We wanted to be good employers, so we offered paid lunches, benefits, bonuses, and raises. What we didn't know was what the total cost of all these expenses. Because of the paid lunches, raises, and bonuses, we pushed our payroll into the realm where the Employer Health Tax came into play. Basically, if you're doing well enough to employ people and pay them a decent wage, the Canadian government adds another tax to your business. This translated into benefits costing us, as the owner's portion, over fifty thousand dollars yearly, after all the applications were processed. The cost of the extended health benefits and the Employer Health Tax, plus the added bonuses and raises, cost the company over one hundred thousand dollars more per year. We failed to do our homework, and, in turn, made the business wealth, our personal wealth, and security of both much weaker. We were both trying to be good employers, but instead, we harmed the business.

DO A BACKGROUND CHECK

Owning a business as the sole owner is ideal if you can handle the responsibility, but at times, we need partners. However, as my father-in-law says, "partnerships are poor ships to sail on," so before you get into a partnership agreement, take a few steps to protect yourself and find out as much as possible about the other people that will be involved.

You need qualified people to ensure their business plans and values align with yours. A proper background check costs money, but may provide you information that your potential partner is hiding to present as a suitable match in that venture. The cost is worth every cent because it protects you and gives you peace of mind as you move forward. If a prospective partner has claimed to have owned businesses prior to offering to go into business with you, find out as much as you can about those businesses. Find out if that person has had partners, whether the previous business was a success, why the person left, and finally, call previous partners. If all ended well, they will have nothing bad to say and may offer positive insights that will help you work with their former partner. If it ended badly, you may discover why it ended, how it ended, and what their impression of this individual is professionally and personally.

Check the prospective partner's credit and, as much as you can, his or her finances. This may seem cynical, but it is important. If this individual is having or has had money trouble in the past, try to uncover why they did, whether the situation was resolved, and, if so, how. There are many legitimate reasons for people to go through tough times, and people with true character can and will give you an honest answer and show why they have the resolve to turn it around.

Unfortunately, a good salesperson can sound a lot like an honest person, so checking won't hurt. If someone is constantly in debt, living off credit, and always seeming to be a victim, dig deeper. If you feel this *victim* has not learned from their mistakes and is unlikely to ever do so, don't risk your financial life. If people are living on credit without a legitimate reason, they are probably looking to maintain that lifestyle, which could very well be at your expense. You may even learn that such a person is simply a liar and a con artist. At the very worst, sidestepping a bad future partner is preferable to having to be perpetually checking up on a skeezy partner.

Further, if you do wind up in a partnership, be sure you plan and know the rights and responsibilities of any directors or other designations, and why those people have been selected. If you are a director, you need to be aware of the responsibilities that accompany that position. A quick conversation with a business lawyer and accountant will clear that up for you. This conversation with your lawyer and accountant should take place before you start anything as a business or a partnership because once business is underway, it can be close to impossible to change. As Bob Sugar says in the movie *Jerry Maguire*, "It's not show friends, it's show business."

HOLDING COMPANY

If you plan to venture into other investments, a holding company is a must. Most big investors with multiple businesses have a holding company to hold the shares of their corporations. This arrangement allows for many options, including investing under corporate laws and rules, which helps you to defer taxes or to maximize personal wealth by taking advantage of the system in place.

If you have a partner, as I did, and that partner wants to be a big spender, as mine did, the holding company can protect you. Unfortunately, I didn't have this protection. This protection is not necessarily needed if you own your business, but if you do have a business partner, have your holding company own your shares in the company.

In my situation, if I had done this, when my ex-partner wanted more money to spend for himself via a dividend, I could have had my dividend paid to my holding company. This would have kept my income tax at the corporate rate, instead of the much higher personal rate, and it would have created savings that could be used as needed. This strategy allows you to invest, save, or defer payments if you have a partner who wants to take out money personally. It also gives you investment options and shelters that are not allotted to personal accounts. Let your money build in this account, taking only what you need personally, if any of it at all. Again, a good accountant can explain the cost and benefits of a holding company, how it will help, and if one is necessary in your situation.

LIFE INSURANCE

A whole life insurance policy can be advantageous for corporations. It has a high premium, on which you can pause the payments if cash flow is insufficient, but it also has a high payout if something happens to you. It is also set up as a before-tax expense, which reduces your corporate income tax. You can borrow it back if need be for emergencies or other reasons. This was a benefit that I used to help me through the months I needed cash after my ex-partner violated the legal agreement. I went to the agent who had set me up with this policy for advice. When he heard what was happening, he agreed to my request for one hundred percent of the payable amount back to me. I received approximately ninety-five thousand dollars, which, in turn, bought me five months to get vendors repaid and keep my business open. You can cancel the policy after you cash it out if you really need to. Speak to people from a reputable company who know exactly how the policy works and to your accountant to be sure what you are offered is legitimate. This may be a great investment for you, as it was for me.

PAY YOURSELF AN AVERAGE SALARY

Because your company makes five hundred thousand dollars profit doesn't mean you need to take all that for yourself. Pay yourself only what you need to live, at least for the first five profitable years. This policy may mean you actually work seven years or longer because it may take a couple years of operating a business before it becomes profitable, but this gives you time to plan your income and investments. Remember that personal income is taxed at a higher rate, both the initial income and some investment income, than corporate income. So, personal income only helps you personally. Banks see your company's value and will apply that to your personal plans if you want to borrow or make plans on the personal side that require proof of income. Having hundreds of thousands of dollars in a personal account only makes the bank a healthy return. Having a strong thriving business with cash reserves can help your business but can also help you personally.

PLAN YEARS AHEAD

Sit with a good accountant and discuss your plans to increase your personal wealth. Start here, and he or she will explain tax implications, advise who to speak with, and how to protect yourself.

Not doing this came back to haunt me on a couple of occasions. One occurred when I was splitting from my ex-partner and I was penalized with personal and corporate income tax to the tune of one hundred and thirty thousand dollars. A second time happened when I was building the fourplex. I had not set up the HST number correctly and did not understand how the rebate system on new builds worked. In both situations, a good accountant could have explained it thoroughly within a twenty-minute meeting.

Set a realistic plan and stick to it; then, as your business income increases, reset your plan and budget with advice from your accountant. If you plan to sell stocks, an income property, or anything that makes you a profit, you will need to account for capital gains tax. I had to sell my income property, for which I made approximately two hundred fifty thousand dollars profit, to pay off three hundred thousand dollars of debt. Unfortunately for me, this sale meant that I owed seventy-five thousand dollars to the government in capital gains tax.

REAL ESTATE

When you have reached the financial age to purchase your first bit of real estate, don't buy your forever home as soon as you can. Real estate can be a great investment or a financial cancer. Buy something that can be turned into an income property later, and do the same with the next one. If you can do this once or twice more before moving into your forever home, even better.

If you don't want to be a landlord, buy a small house or building and upgrade it slightly a few times. You will pay the same as you would in rent or close to that amount, but you will also get capital gains to help move to the next step. If you want to be a landlord or want to try it, have multiple units to secure your financial needs. This can work well provided you do not max them out constantly for personal gain, but if you do, use most of that money to further your portfolio and personal wealth, including keeping the units up to date and clean.

Real estate appreciates, for the most part, and this means that you will have others paying your mortgage down for you, while the property value is increasing. It might take longer to buy your forever home, but when you do, you will be able to afford a nice home and still have income but for leisure. However, as mentioned above regarding capital gains taxes, factor the taxes into your long-term plan. As of now, if a property is your primary residence, you pay no capital gains tax on the profit of a sale. Also, learn about mortgage rates and property tax for residential versus commercial properties. If you don't understand these distinctions, you could pay more than expected and make a low return on investment (ROI). For example, commercial interest rates are currently three percent higher than residential rates, which could equal four to five hundred dollars per month. However, you can write your interest rate off of an income property. Your property taxes will be lower for residential, which increases monthly cash flow, and you need a smaller down payment to purchase a residential property. The question to ask is, do you need the cash flow immediately? And what is your end goal for the investment? Again, do your homework and get professional advice on your plan from start to finish before you jump into a situation that could turn regrettable.

LEASING

When looking for a bricks-and-mortar location, consider a few things prior to opening. First, leasehold improvements can be very costly. The improvements stay with the owner; you cannot take flooring, paint, windows, or almost anything you put into that unit with you when you leave. Before renting a place that needs work, look for places that have already been renovated and are *turnkey*.

I did not follow this advice at one of my first locations. I really wanted an office in my hometown of Stratford, Ontario, and I wanted it to be impressive. I didn't look at much but found a new building that had come up for lease; however, it was an open-concept store that needed to be split into multiple units. I didn't negotiate any allowance from the owners and was held responsible to pay for all the improvements. These improvements cost over sixty thousand dollars to complete, and I had far more space than I needed. I thought it would be easy to sub-lease some rooms to other practitioners, but I never contacted others or confirmed this option as a possibility. I had to move out within six months because I could not afford the cost of rent—all my money had gone to renovations, which now made it easy for someone else to have a turnkey operation and a beautiful unit at my expense. I then found a turnkey unit that cost one thousand dollars less a month; we stayed there for the next eight years. If I had followed my own advice right at the start, I would have started my business with money to support our operational needs versus bootstrapping the first year. I would have been sixty thousand dollars richer, which could have paid for a lot of operating costs at that time.

Second, before signing a lease, take the time to call the fire marshal, an electrician, a plumber, the building inspector, and check the zoning requirements. If you plan to do some work yourself, these professionals will usually consult with you for a minimal cost, but such consultation could save you a fortune. Have them check the facility for anything that is not up to code or that will need work. Sometimes, you have a great vision of what something could be, but an inspector may not agree, and you could end up ceasing your plans due to by-laws or permit issues. This is the time to speak with the landlord and get the work done by that person. If you move in and sign a lease, you may quickly find out that your unit is not up to code. Although this is the responsibility of the building owner to correct, you could have your doors locked and the business shut down or be forced to pay for the improvements yourself. The price of getting legal advice, then possibly suing the owner could drain your finances before a court decision is reached. Further, the cost to your reputation and business momentum could be worse than any financial losses you sustain at that unit.

Again, I didn't follow this advice, mostly out of desperation. I moved into a new location, thinking that I would make some changes and have a showroom as well as a manufacturing area in the back, and I'd pay less rent per month than where I was. We moved in, signed a lease, and started doing work. Then reality hit. I needed to do five thousand dollars of electrical work to bring the unit up to code and run my machines. I was asked to put a fire break on the ceiling because there were apartments above, and the fire code stated there must be one installed, which would cost another one thousand, five hundred dollars. The savings I thought I was going to have by moving there were then used up, and expenses were exceeded before we were there for three months.

Third, when it comes time to sign a lease, negotiate and use a lawyer who is an expert in that area of law. Then the landlord cannot add clauses to the lease that put you in peril if something goes wrong. Also, have your lawyer amend the lease so you are comfortable with it; start by removing a personal guarantee. If there is a personal guarantee in the lease and you have to close your business, the landlord can come after you personally for the loss in rent. This could force you into personal bankruptcy and leave you in a dire situation. Even if you were at a location for a decade and paid half the landlord's mortgage for them, a landlord is in no way responsible to grant leniency about collecting money to which they are legally entitled. You will be surprised how quickly most landlords agree to most of your terms because they want the unit leased. The lease you sign helps them secure financing, if they need it, as most do, or secure the return they expect to get from the investment. If you run into a landlord who won't budge on anything, consider it a big red flag. If someone won't be flexible to get your business, he or she is not apt to be flexible if something goes wrong. Simply walk away; there are a lot of spaces out there. Sometimes the best deals you make are the deals you don't.

HAVE A CUSTOMER BASE

Never rely on family and friends to be your customer base, no matter how popular you think you are or how large your family is. In certain industries, this is more important than in others; however, it still applies to all businesses. If you believe that you can make a go or even start a business by relying on the support of your family and friends, just don't do it. I have a very large family, over one hundred adults when all are tallied. When I was starting my venture in the orthotics industry, I made them aware, with the help of my parents, of what I was doing and how they could benefit from my services. Some came in to see me if they needed or wanted the services I provided. Others did not, not because they didn't care to help but because they didn't require those services, or they already had someone they trusted to provide similar services. It wasn't their responsibility to make my business a success. There must be a need or a want for any services. If you cannot provide a wanted service, product, or deal, people cannot be expected to spend their hard-earned money to make you successful.

The best example I can give is when I was twenty-one years old and working in a restaurant in Stratford. Stratford is a small town where everyone knows each other for the most part. I was hired mostly because I went to school with the manager and had known the family for as long as I could remember. The restaurant provided good food, beer, and wine; it had a decent atmosphere, and it was in a great location for both the early theatre crowd and the crowd looking for some entertainment at night. The dinner crowd was always steady during the theatre season, and the restaurant was usually busy at night then as well. However, when winter came, the crowd thinned out drastically. The owner sponsored his men's league hockey team and tried many different promotions to get busier dinners, especially on weekends, and he relied strongly on friends and family to support the enterprise. I found that most did for a while, stopping in for a drink here and there, but in the end, what was offered wasn't as good as at other places in town. I don't mean the food or beverages weren't as good; I mean the total package wasn't. Even friends and family were more inclined to patronize places that met their wants for that day or evening. Had this restaurant met their needs and wants, not only would the owner's friends and family have wanted to frequent the establishment more, but many others in town would have too. Then, they would have had a successful place that was consistent and profitable. Unfortunately, the restaurant were forced to close after a few years. Like a true entrepreneur, the owner learned from his mistakes and has had some great success in other industries over the years. Thankfully, this failure was just a bump in the road for him.

SAFETY NET

While it may be difficult to assess how much money is needed as a safety net at first, you need to know what your break-even points are and what your monthly fixed costs total. For example, if your business expenses total twenty thousand dollars a month, your break-even point is not just the twenty thousand dollars it costs for one month's operation, it is a minimum of sixty thousand dollars. You need to cover a downturn of fifty to seventy percent, and four to six months of expenses, so you do not put serious financial pressure on your business and hence on yourself.

The COVID-19 pandemic provides a dramatic example of how unstable a number of small businesses were. Two months into the pandemic, many businesses were preparing to close, and in three months, many more were preparing to or closing their businesses. A safety net is not easy to factor or assess, and it requires a lot of discipline to develop as a strategy. It's hard looking at all that cash and knowing it represents zero dollars at that moment. You may need to use it for extenuating reasons like a downturn or other cash flow issues; however, if you can maintain this strategy, you will have created a strong safety net. At first, my ex-business partner agreed to and followed this rule. However, as we became more successful, he started wanting more personal material goods and slowly kept taking more and more out of that nest of money. Subsequently, when we split and he had a downturn, he was out of money in a month, leading to his bankruptcy.

Exit plan

An exit plan is especially important if you do enter into a partnership. However, exit plans don't mean just selling; they may also mean changing plans, investing, venturing into other industries, or retiring. The exit plan will show you where you want to be in the future. When another large company wanted to buy my former business, for example, I couldn't sell my shares because my ex-partner had to approve the sale. Had I had a partnership agreement with a planned exit, I could have forced a sale of the business for over two million dollars, which would have meant we each could realize more than one million dollars after tax. If that sale had happened, the finances received would have secured my plans to invest in another industry safely. I would have been under forty years old and had money to advance and to continue with a few projects with which I am currently involved.

Hopefully, you're in an industry and have tangible assets or a reputation that makes it worth someone's while to buy your business when you want out, but some businesses do not have that luxury. My brother, for example, is a mason with a successful business; that means that he *is* the business. His reputation and construction development are his security, and his skills are his equity. He has limited equipment and employs tradespeople who can leave his company and join another at any moment. That poses a problem for small construction, renovation companies, and most trades; all of them make up the assets of their business. It is cheaper for someone to buy the necessary equipment, price prospective jobs competitively, and build a reputation, than it is to buy someone else's business. There are exceptions, but unless you are a big outfit with a lot of equipment, a customer base, and continuous contracts, you may never get anyone to pay you for the business you've built. In cases like this, planning for retirement has to be a priority and part of your business plan and execution, which is always harder to achieve than it seems. Personally, I try to run my business so I could effectively sell it at any moment if the right opportunity arises. You don't want to spend time trying to backtrack. That lesson cost me far more than it should have.

There is nothing more effective than a sound plan that is executed to the best of a person's ability. Things will change, sometimes quickly, and at times, these shifts are mandated by short-term success or temporary failure. Having a plan allows for change while simultaneously keeping your end goals in view. I have always liked the saying, "Plan your work, then work your plan." When I renovated my new location, I was in a position where I could afford the material or the labour, but not both. Luckily, I have an uncle who is recently retired from a major construction company. He was kind enough to do the work for no pay, just to help me, earning my sincere gratitude. I hope I can find a way to repay him one day.

My uncle's commitment also illustrated an important lesson in being prepared. He came in, measured everything, did scaled drawings, and came back to check on changes and to tape the ground for the layout. He planned each day and prepared the job with the care and miniscule mindset he had used building hospitals, bridges (including one spanning across the Canada/USA border), and shopping centres. The job was done perfectly, but seeing the extensive time that he spent in preparation made me rethink how I train my staff and think about how his method of time management could help us. This constituted another lesson learned by watching someone with a wealth of knowledge and experience. I once read that it is better to have lightning in the hand than thunder in the mouth; in this case, it definitely applied.

CHAPTER 6

TRUST

Trust is something someone may need to earn or may receive through the benefit of the doubt, but either way, it is something that can evaporate rapidly in the light of a few simple actions. You need to have trust, but not blind trust *carte blanche*. Trust in business means that you have to be prepared that some people will look out for themselves, that for some people, money supersedes all else. Everyone feels like they are the good guy, but if someone can con you, they will. A quick con can deplete you financially and sink your business and your personal wealth completely, and the emotional stress you and your family may be put through can bankrupt you in other ways. Practiced con artists are hard to spot, at least initially. But once you see them for who they are, all the red flags present themselves. Here are eight facts about con artists, and the people who become them, based on Maria Konnikova's *The Confidence Game*:

1. **Con artists aren't obvious villains.** One review of almost six hundred cases of company fraud found that approximately forty percent of the fraudsters were considered *highly respected* by their co-workers. This demonstrates how convincing con artists are. When you see a highly respected business person, it doesn't necessarily follow that they have achieved that success and reputation ethically or morally (Konnikova 33).

2. **Psychologists have identified traits that seem to predispose people to be suited to be con artists:** *1.* manipulative; *2.* deceitful; *3.* aggressive; *4.* shameless. They also found that it takes the right circumstances for these people to become con artists (Konnikova 22, 24).

3. **Con artists take advantage of people's inclination to trust someone.** According to an Oxford University study, trust makes people happier, but also more vulnerable. They believe that those who trust do better, and those who trust more become the ideal, albeit unwilling, victim of the confidence game (Allchin).

4. **Con artists are masters at reading people and appealing to their perceived exceptionalism and vanity.** They need to do this to gain their *marks'* trust and confidence in the first place (Konnikova 41-43, 64-65, 179).

5. **Con artists' greatest strength can also be their greatest weakness.** Their extreme confidence, which they use as a weapon, can also be their downfall (275-279).

6. **They are not pathological liars who lie out of compulsion.** The con artist's lie is calculated, strategic, and related to a plan moving forward (Konnikova 117).

7. **Con artists benefit from technological advances.** Konnivoka points out that consumer fraud has risen by 60 percent since 2008 (10).

8. **Most con artists get away with their cons.** It's commonly thought that only foolish people get conned. So, it's understandable that most people who are conned don't want to admit they have fallen victim to a con artist and don't report the con to the authorities. Therefore, most cons are never brought to trial (Konnikova 11, 16, 190).

Con artists, then, can be nearly invisible—their social camouflage is excellent, so be vigilant and place trust only after it is earned.

Being prepared with legal paperwork for possible conning is smart and well worth the money. If you draft a fair agreement, a reasonable person will live up to that agreement and accept the consequences if they don't, so in the end, there is no damage done when you have a properly analyzed legal document in place. Be wary of anyone who tries to avoid signing anything or uses your trust to manipulate you into something that gives them an advantage over you.

When I was meeting with prospective buyers for my fourplex, I mentioned in conversation that I was looking for someone to install my guard and handrails. The people to whom I was speaking are reputable guys and were looking to help me. They had recently heard of someone who seemed to be an authority about getting quality rails done at an attractive rate. They sent me his contact information, and I met him at the site for a consultation. He was running late, and I had a forty-minute wait. When he did arrive, he told me that since he didn't want to be late meeting me—because he believed so thoroughly in the value of other people's time—he had been speeding and was pulled over. He added that, after talking to the officer, he gained a new client. During this first meeting, he spoke a lot about how much money he had, vacations he went on, his cars, and his multiple homes. This seemed insecure, but harmless, and he knew what he was talking about in terms of railings and their installation. Because he had been recommended by others whom I trusted, I thought that he was a legitimate contractor, and I let his off-putting comments slide.

He contacted me later that night, saying that he would have something for me in the next couple of days, which was a fairly normal response. We spoke again, and he asked if I had any contacts in the construction industry in the London area. Since I knew a few salesmen who dealt with some large construction companies and a couple of owners of some big construction companies, I responded that I did. He then offered to do my job at a reduced rate if I could introduce him to these people. I agreed. This wasn't a red flag to me because he was trying to get his name known in the London area. If I could help and he could still make some money from my job, I felt we both benefitted. He started sending multiple texts of his work which looked promising, but then, he began asking if I played sports and if I could help him meet some people connected to sports. I found this odd but thought that if he was new in town, maybe he was just trying to build his network. We agreed on a price for the railing job, and he asked for a deposit. Again, this was a normal request, so I obliged. He told me that it would take four to six weeks to complete the job and was excited to get this job done for me. Then the red flags started to appear.

During the first few weeks, I invited him to lunch to meet some promising contacts, but he either didn't respond or he cancelled the day of each lunch. He texted less and less and was not returning messages. I did finally reach him; on that day, he invited me to meet him at a Starbucks to discuss how the rails were coming. During this meeting, I got a handwritten invoice from him, and we discussed the installation, which he told me would take two and a half more weeks. At this time, he inquired about what I did professionally and why I had bought the property, and I explained. At this point, I still didn't think of him negatively. He went into a story about how his first company was stolen from him by a tricky business partner. He emphasized that he had contacted all the clients who had not received their product they had paid for and that he promised them all that he would either repay their deposits or finish their job at no additional cost. I sympathized with him, being in the middle of my issues with my ex-partner. We left with a handshake.

During that meeting, I also asked if he dealt with a company that could do the engineered drawings that the city required for the permit. He said he did and asked me to pass the cost of the drawings to him, and he would take care of it. After that meeting, things started going very wrong. I texted him two and a half weeks later to see how the work was going, and his response read, "Two and a half more weeks." I didn't hear from him for another week, so I texted again, and again he responded with, "Two and half more weeks." I asked about the drawings, and he said that he had just spoken with the authorities and that we should hear back any time.

I was becoming worried, so the following day, I texted him more than once but got no response. I tried calling but received an automated response saying that this number was not assigned. Now, I was angry and wanted answers immediately. Luckily, he had previously texted me his address—to impress me with the area he claimed to be living in. My wife, seeing the state of anger I was in, drove me over. After driving to the address and not finding him, I left a message with a young woman there who knew him and who volunteered that he had not finished a railing job for her. I issued the ultimatum that my next communication would be through the police. The bigger problem was my tenants being unable to live in their units, which was costing three thousand and three hundred dollars monthly in rent revenue because the city could not issue me occupancy permits for units that were deemed unsafe.

Finally, I called the London Police Services financial crime department to make a report. I had learned another valuable lesson on how liar's work and how calculated a con artist is. I discovered that no matter what the amount of the deposit is, the type of work involved, or the time it steals from you, you cannot press charges if the contractor gives you a date by which they will finish the work. It doesn't matter how many times that person doesn't show to do the work. Providing a date shows intent to finish the job, which avoids any police involvement. In cases like this one, if you choose to pursue getting compensated, it will become a civil matter and could take years to get any monies back, and you might receive just more stress. Seasoned con artists know all about legal loopholes. Here are some tips to avoid being taken advantage of:

- Get legal contracts written up, and do not just automatically agree to their contracts; be sure you're protected.
- Use trust accounts for deposits. This requires contractors do the work to get paid.
- Have penalties for work not completed in due time and/or done improperly.

If you don't make sure you know who you're dealing with, trust you will be taken advantage of.

Chapter 7

A Done Deal

In 2012, I was sitting in one of London's most famous establishments, Joe Kools. I have patronized this establishment many times over the years and have gotten to know most of the other regular clients. Jeffy Bialkoski, who is a professional musician, sat in my booth with me to see the onstage act. We started chatting, and our conversation led into a discussion of an invention of his. He had been contracted to play a St. Patrick's Day event when his bass player informed him a few nights before the date that he couldn't do the gig. St. Patrick's Day is a big money-maker for musicians who play professionally in bars, which meant that talented players were already spoken for at this point, and the chances of finding someone to play on such short notice was nearly impossible.

Jeffy is interesting and one of the best guitar players I have ever seen play. He is a master of the instrument physically, but he excels in music theory. He has played in numerous bands since the age of fourteen, most notably as the lead guitarist for *Bob Noxious*, a local London talent.

Without a bass player, the Irish music fit for the occasion wouldn't sound right, and he was rightfully worried that he would be penalized by the bar owner if the gig did not go well, since only his name was on the contract. However, with his knowledge of guitars and all their accessories, Jeffy came up with an ingenious modification to his guitar. He simply attached another pickup, a device that takes the sound and sends it to an amplifier so that it's audible at a much louder level. In this case, the second pickup was built into the hole of the guitar where the strings run over, but it was built horizontally, so it captured only the low E and A strings. This pickup connected separately to a different input and amplifier, with the aid of a octave pedal, so the only sound coming out of that speaker was from the E and A strings one octave lower. The E and A strings are commonly known as the bass strings, and usually a bass plays the same notes but an octave lower to give the music a deeper, stronger sound, essential for a St. Patrick's Day repertoire. Jeff described this modification to me and I had to see it, so I arranged to go to his house and get a demonstration from him.

He went through it all with me very clearly, and he let me play around on the guitar for a bit. I am an amateur but can play well. One of my favourite artist's songs thrives with bass notes. I played a few riffs, turning the pickup on and off as he had shown me, and I could not only hear, but feel, the difference it made. This modification could make anyone sound significantly better, whether they were an amateur or a professional. I realized that he had discovered something that could be scaled worldwide. I made a deal with him: I would finance everything, and he could decide what percentage that was worth. To his credit, Jeffy said he would only do a deal if it was an equal split. We agreed and got a business account and arrangement setup. He showed me a few other acoustic guitars with which he had also experimented with the pickup modification, as well as his plans for an electric guitar.

Later, while I was working in Ottawa, I went for dinner. Being alone and bored, I opened up Facebook because I cannot ignore that little red notification on the app. I opened the app, clicked the notification, and saw that Jeffy had tagged me in his post that announced that we had been accepted to be on *Dragons' Den*. Jeffy went to the auditions for the show in secret. He waited hours in line and pitched the instrument to the judges at the audition. He kept this secret from everyone until he was notified that he had impressed the judges, and they had advanced him to pitch the invention on the show. At that time, they informed him of the date, time frame, and location of the audition taping, which he then posted on Facebook and tagged me in that post. We would be filming March 23, 2013, but we wouldn't know when it would be aired until the editing was completed. We worked for the next couple of months on improving the guitars, on a name, and on a sales pitch for the show.

We were scheduled to be at the CBC building at 6:00 a.m. in downtown Toronto on the day of shooting. Jeffy and I decided to go down the night before and stay in a hotel, so we would be fresh when we arrived. The night was restless and morning came quickly. I didn't have my usual breakfast, so we wouldn't be late for our arrival. We walked in with our gear and were received by the *Dragons' Den* CBC staff. We then stood in the lobby awaiting instructions for about forty-five minutes, which felt like hours on an empty and growling stomach. They informed us of the waiver that we needed to sign to participate on the show, and one part of the document stuck out for me. There is a clause that they can edit as they need or want to, meaning, as I understood it, that one dragon could ask a question, but they could edit our answer to a different question when it aired. This was for dramatic effect if they felt they needed it, so what you see on a broadcast may not show what actually happened. They then ushered us to a waiting room.

The green room looked over the Toronto harbour and was filled with complimentary snacks and refreshments that we could partake of until they called for us, which could have been anytime that morning, if at all. While waiting, entertainment was provided on a large screen television, which played only previous seasons of *Dragons' Den*. This was one of the most entertaining moments of this experience. Although no one in the green room had ever been on *Dragons' Den*, each was quick to criticize previous guests and to offer their opinion on what the previous participants should have done.

Once we were called, we were led down to the staging area to get microphones attached to our shirts and have the rules of the show explained. We walked across the catwalk and down the stairs and into a room, where we finally met the dragons. We had a few false starts when the stage crew would interrupt us and have us start over. Our plan was to demonstrate and describe the instrument and, if the opportunity presented itself, have Kevin O'Leary come down and play the guitar himself. I had researched each dragon and made an assumption that Kevin would be our best dragon with whom to do this sort of business.

Jeffy jumped right in and started the pitch, describing the instrument and playing some riffs for them, so they could hear how it worked. Because Kevin O'Leary is a true guitar fan, we really wanted him to play and feel this instrument. He asked if he could, and we obliged because we thought he would understand the scope, and he did.

The questions started, and I took over. We discussed our patent and our plan. We really didn't want to use the money for stock and marketing, but the rules of the show dictate that you must ask for something. The cost to build a guitar company from the ground up and compete with the current manufacturers was beyond us. We asked for eighteen thousand dollars for thirty percent of the company, both very irrelevant. What we really wanted was an introduction to the prestigious guitar manufacturers and to try to get a licence agreement. Once we answered the questions to the best of our knowledge, the advice rolled in. Jeffy and I had discussed this part previously; our plan was to have them lead us to what they thought was the best solution. In my experience in life and business, people always believe their ideas and advice are superior and should be followed. If we had one of the dragons give us advice about how a licence agreement was the best option, they would be more likely to offer a deal, which is what happened. All five dragons liked the idea and commented that they would make an offer, but none had the contacts that Kevin had in the guitar world. Kevin offered us a deal with one big contingency: Fender had to sign on or the deal became void. We accepted, and Kevin's due diligence started immediately after we walked off the stage. Kevin's assistant had us fill out paperwork on our past and present financial situations as well as information about the company. The paperwork consisted of multiple pages and was very thorough, which was a first for me, an experience that left an impression as to its importance.

Our pitch was recorded in March, but it was not aired until December of the same year. When we were on stage presenting, we were out there for approximately thirty minutes. When the episode aired, we got less than three minutes of air time. What the viewers of *Dragons' Den* didn't see is the mass of minutiae that were disregarded for their lack of entertainment value. This opportunity offered an important life lesson on presentations. During the pitch, Kevin said he would fly us on his private jet to California to meet the upper level of Fender. After the recording, we found out what pickups and components Fender was already licensed to use, and we made our prototypes with those pickups and components to two modified Fender guitars, one acoustic and one electric, for the pitch in California. We felt as if we had won the lottery, and knowing the importance of hearing and feeling the guitar, we were confident the Fender guys would understand and accept Jeffy's modifications.

At the time, Fender did approximately eight hundred million dollars in sales yearly, so we were hoping they would put our system into approximately ten percent of their guitars, and we hoped that they offered a royalty of one to two percent on the sales. If they awarded us even one percent, and sold ten million dollars' worth of those products worldwide, we would receive one hundred thousand dollars yearly for the idea, but it was quite possible that they could do fifty million dollars or more in yearly sales. Nothing is ever guaranteed, but this was possibly an enormous life-changing moment for us, so we couldn't help but feel overwhelmingly excited.

Unfortunately, nothing happened. We were never put on a private jet and flown out to California. Kevin's assistant wanted a video, which would not do the instrument justice. Fender passed on the project, and we had nothing moving forward. I got caught up in the process of the recording and the advice given to us from the producers at CBC, who were all very generous with their advice from experiences in the past. I also got caught up in the excitement of the opportunity.

After the recording, we drove back to London from Toronto, discussing the possibilities of the next steps. We were told that traffic on our website the night the pitch aired could increase by five thousand times, and that typically meant sales would roll in. I was worried about customer service and thought that, if we had a lot of orders, we would want to get the guitars to the customers as soon as possible. I invested in having two hundred and fifty guitars made and ready for the night of the airing, and I set up an e-commerce site with payment options. We had a lot of interest, but because we didn't get the right type of e-commerce site set up, we had no real sales.

So, out of excitement, I increased my investment from ten thousand dollars to sixty thousand dollars, which I have never completely gotten back to this day, although we did sell all the guitars. Had I gotten the site set up far in advance and tested it, we might have made our money back that very night, but we will never know because we lost all the information when the site crashed.

A deal is not done when there is a proposal of an agreement; it's not done when the papers are signed to pursue the proposal. It's done when the cheque you receive is deposited into your account, and the cheque clears, then the money has become yours.

CHAPTER 8

KEEP YOUR EMOTIONS OUT OF IT

One of my most repeated and greatest mistakes is allowing my emotions to get the best of me and cloud my judgement. When I finally separated from my ex-partner from Ottawa, I was excited and looking forward to the future. I had a sound projected income; I had full control of my business and was ready to start developing products to bring to market in that industry. This is also the time I made more than one emotional decision that could have resulted in the closure of my business and could have forced me and my wife into bankruptcy. Bankruptcy can happen unbelievably quickly once you hit the tipping point.

At the time, my ex-partner was living by his agreement, largely, and we were just ending the fifth month of a thirty-six-month agreement at the start of June 2018. My youngest daughter wasn't one year old yet and loved to wake up around seven every morning. My oldest daughter would sleep a bit later, but she was usually tangled up or wrapped around her mother.

It wasn't much of a gesture, but most mornings I would, at that time of year, take my youngest out for a walk in our neighbourhood for a couple of hours. It was for me as much as for her. I listened to music, let my mind run wild—thinking over new ideas and admired the development that was happening in our area of town. I kept walking past a vacant double lot that had both houses already torn down. I really thought having that property in a revitalizing part of town and investing in our neighbourhood would constitute a really good move. However, my ex-partner wanted a dividend taken from the cash accounts as of December 31, 2017, the day we were finally separated legally as business partners to close the deal. The problem with having the money come out as a dividend was that we would have to pay personal income tax on it. An even bigger problem was that that money had to go back into the business to pay business expenses, as our accountant and lawyers had instructed us to expect. I wasn't sure what the personal tax implications would be, but I figured I could handle them.

Through my excitement, I started making all the changes I wanted to. I started with an online e-commerce store and invested in developing CNC machines to mill orthotics that could cut both plastic and rubber, which would be the only ones on the market at that time because others just cut rubber. I was consulting and flying out west to help a clinic while they used my manufacturing. I changed our benefit plan and instituted some raises. The money that I was projected to make was in excess of three hundred and fifty thousand dollars, so these expenses seemed like nothing in comparison. I didn't wait, but went in full throttle, fuelled by past frustration and present excitement. I thought that the business could be rebuilt to its former glory. At the time of negotiations with my ex-partner, the business had a value of over two million dollars.

To put those negotiations in the proper context, the one clinic in Ottawa was responsible for half the value of the entire business, so for him to keep the other two meant that he should have paid me six hundred thousand dollars. Through months of negotiations, it eventually came to light that he couldn't make such a purchase because he had insufficient credit, equity, or cash to pay the difference. This fact also explained why he couldn't buy the entire business at eight hundred thousand dollars when I offered him the opportunity to buy me out and why he would not sell for market value; he was severely overleveraged. To move this dissolving of the partnership forward, we made an agreement that required no transfer of cash. However, my ex-partner had to agree to use my manufacturing for three years, at an agreed markup, which would make up the difference of value that I had in the other half of the company. I had only one protection in the agreement, which stated that if he violated the agreement, he would owe me ten thousand dollars per month for the duration of the agreement. That alone constituted a risk because he could have violated the agreement from the beginning and paid three hundred and sixty thousand dollars for six hundred thousand dollars' worth of value. Fortunately, he didn't realize that. What I didn't expect was for him not to pay his bills for the first forty-five days, even though the agreement clearly stated fifteen days, and then to pay only partial amounts. That would be the trend for the rest of the time we did business. I later learned that my ex-partner did not put the dividend money back into his business account to pay his bills; instead, the funds went to personal expenses and luxuries. Additionally, he approached an employee of mine with an offer to work for him on a part-time basis, which was another violation of the agreement.

In late April of that year, I contacted my lawyer to speak to these issues and to see if the agreement included anything that would allow me to recoup losses and redress these infractions. During our discussion, I asked if we should just offer that he pay me four hundred thousand dollars, so he would be free and clear, and we would accept nothing lower than the monthly penalty to which he had agreed in the separation contract. I didn't have the lawyer send the email at that time to suggest these solutions because I felt I would have lost; pride got in the way of my logical thinking and functioning with a business frame of mind. Instead, I kept sticking it out and dealing with the issues he was causing, believing that the situation would get better and that the more than three hundred and fifty thousand dollars projected yearly profit would make it worthwhile. By the time we proposed the offer he was being investigated for unacceptable business practices by his major insurance provider, which he was advised not to consider if he became de-listed he wouldn't have had business to worry about. We also learn, after he had filed personal bankruptcy on April 4, 2019, that he had created another business, which was another violation of the agreement. This manoeuvre effectively redirected customers and used vendors directly to increase his profit and decrease mine.

In late April 2018, I received that *little brown envelope* from the Canada Revenue Agency, informing me that I owed over ninety-eight thousand dollars in personal income taxes from the year before, mostly because of the dividends that I had received when the split was finalized. This income stemmed from undeclared dividends because my ex-partner hadn't signed the paperwork to shift my shares over to my holding company as I had requested four years prior. Clearly, I should have followed up and made sure that he had done the paperwork properly. With my accountant sorting out the books and my lawyer trying to set up the holding company and explaining it all to me and to my ex-business partner, it slipped past us. I didn't provide them with the signed paperwork. The 2018 letter from CRA caused me serious anxiety, such as I had never really had to deal with in my life, but I believed I could come up with a solution.

One morning as I was walking with my daughter Grace, I kept looking at that property, and, ironically enough, a sign went up listing it for sale. When I looked into the listing, all the approved drawings, permits, and development thus far were being offered within the sale, which would save me a year to two of mortgage payments while I waited to get my own drawings completed and approved by the city. I called a friend who was a real estate agent, which proved to be another error that was based on emotional thinking. I assumed that it was a vacant lot. I thought, how hard could it be to get the deal done? Because of that miscalculation and using a friend instead of someone who had expertise specific to this situation, the offer was rushed. We were bullied into the price and many clauses and promises that were made verbally ended up being omitted from the paper offer, which later cost me time, and therefore, money.

Before making the offer, I went to a friend and told him my plan, showed him the limited drawings we were allowed to keep, and discussed a projected timeline. My friend agreed to lend me the one hundred thousand dollars, with interest, to pay off my taxes so I could be approved by the bank and make an offer on the property. Even with interest, I would be ahead by not having to take the money out of my business and paying personal tax on that withdrawal from the business. We moved speedily, and, in mid-June 2018, I had an accepted offer from the other party. I had to decide how to get this build done efficiently, so I pay the loan and interest back to my friend. In August of that year I discovered that my ex-partner was violating our agreement by planning to stop using my manufacturing; in effect, he was trying to increase his profits by not paying me. At this point, I was desperate, scared, and worried that I would be unable to realize my goals, and that I might just be getting into even deeper trouble, yet I also had confidence that this was a good move and was a sound investment. This was a very strange feeling to be struggling with. Had I made the offer before these incidents we could have settled the agreement and I could have recoverd the six hundred thousand of share value he owed me for my shares of the offices he owned, and would still have owned my offices and manufacturing operations.

I mentioned my plans to a close relative of mine who had been in construction for his entire adult life. The conversation quickly led to a discussion more about a partnership. Unfortunately, my history with this family member, in whom I believed and trusted, proved to be detrimental. I allowed his praise of me and for this project to influence my judgement, and in my enthusiasm for this new venture and in my desperation over my circumstances, I trusted him with too much information. Like a true conman he used that information for his gain. You must always look for real actions, not trust or flattery—this goes for products offered from insurance companies, banks, sales people, or whomever—because people often offer you their product to profit themselves. That doesn't mean that such a strategy is bad or corrupt; that's how business works. It also doesn't mean that you will benefit from the offer or it will help you. Therefore, it's okay to say no.

In my case, my uncle accompanied me when I spoke with the realtor about the property. I showed him the design and asked what he thought it would cost to build prior to making an offer. From the numbers he gave me, which were a pared-down version of another estimate I had gotten, this project looked like a really good investment, even after adding thirty percent to his numbers. I did not understand the importance of little details but assumed my uncle did. Because I lowered my guard, I didn't vet my uncle as I would have if I was going into a venture with anyone else, nor did I push for a written legal agreement prior to getting the offer drawn up. I committed a very costly error.

At the beginning, we agreed that he would do the work he could for five hundred dollars per week, but we did not settle on a percentage of profit. He kept hinting at a fifty-fifty split with no risk assumed on his end. He was to do the work and be on site as the general contractor from start to end. I spoke with him about the percentage of profit he would get and indicated that all invoices were to be paid by my wife and myself directly to the vendors. He agreed to this arrangement, but I could tell he understood that I did not fully trust him.

When he realized I trusted him with the work but not the finances, everything changed. He began suggesting that contracting the work out would be better in the end; clearly, he no longer wanted to do the work himself, something that had been an important piece of the puzzle when deciding to enter into this venture.

While I tried to get an agreement in place after the fact, it became apparent he was hostile to any such arrangement. I had my lawyer draw up an agreement, which released him from everything; he signed this quite quickly and immediately requested copies. Later, when I was going through the bank account after receiving his invoice, I noticed that he had kept over five thousand dollars from an investor. He had never transferred this amount into the bank account we were using for this project. This matter was never satisfactorily resolved.

I had just been through this with my business ex-partner, and I allowed it to happen again. Had I waited and looked at my uncle as if he were a stranger, I wouldn't have rushed into a situation that led to such costly mistakes. It was my responsibility to protect myself and my family and to do the required due diligence to position myself optimally, no matter how well I thought I knew the other party. I needed to think more critically, with more detachment and more strategy, from the offer to the property purchase right through to getting the project finished. My excitement pushed me to rush moves in my manufacturing; my pride stopped me from getting out of a bad deal; my loyalty led me to agree to purchase a property in a deal that did not protect my best interest; and my trust stopped me from doing proper due diligence. I did these things because I allowed my emotions to get in my way, putting myself, my wife, and my children at financial risk.

Had I stepped back, taken my emotions out of the equation, and looked at the larger picture, I would have seen a solution right in front of me. The property in which I had one of my offices included a residential apartment, and was a perfect situation to be altered to a residential triplex. The floor plan is perfect to add another floor and another two-bedroom apartment above and the parking is already acceptable by the city for a residential triplex. The construction cost would have been approximately three hundred thousand dollars for the engineered drawings, permits, and actual completed construction.

London had and continues to have an extremely low vacancy rate, so finding renters usually takes only a day or two to fill units. The work would have taken an estimated six to eight months to finish; at that time, the property could have been refinanced for eighty percent of the total value of the property. Because I hadn't used much of the equity in that building since I purchased it in 2012, I could have turned a bad situation into a massively positive one.

After refinancing the mortgage when the building was turned into a triplex, I would have walked away with more than two hundred and fifty thousand dollars from the new mortgage on the finished triplex, which would have satisfied all my business debts at the time. My wife and I, with renters, could have carried the mortgages on my renovated triplex and the fourplex we built. The profit from the rent of both properties would have paid the mortgage on our marital home, our car payments, and brought us close to being debt free, improving our immediate situation from dire to secure and our future retirement would also have been secure.

These two properties, with half or more of the mortgages paid down by the renters and the value increasing from two to four percent yearly, would have had a combined worth of between three and three and a half million dollars in the next fifteen years. My anxiety and fear got the best of me, and I didn't make an effort to step around them to see the entire picture as I should have. This lapse in judgement haunts me, not only because of what might have been, but because of what I needed it to be. I didn't look at all angles to solve my problems, which proved to be an expensive lesson on how emotions can muddy your thought processes and keep you from succeeding.

CHAPTER 9

WALKING AWAY

Some of the best deals you make are the ones you walk away from. However, someone who has the entrepreneurial instinct often thinks that they can improve on someone else's ideas, systems, or branding to turn mediocrity into greatness, or at the very least, into an opportunity for improvement. When this kind of person hears an idea, his or her mind turns on, and possibilities flood their brain. Many have made fortunes from the most unlikely opportunities that came their way. Nonetheless, ask yourself these questions: if the opportunity is that good, why is another person selling it? What do they get out of the deal? Is this venture going to be a short-term or long-term investment? How much effort and time can you put into making it successful? Does something not add up? Do you have the skill set to do this? Be honest; you owe honesty to yourself and your current business and investments. During my time as an entrepreneur, I have had many opportunities come my way that I have passed on. The ones that really intrigue you are the ones about which you need extreme self-awareness to keep your wits about you.

During the time that I was deeply in debt because of my involvement with my ex-business partner, the fourplex costs skyrocketed, and I spiralled from that moment on. I had an opportunity to become a manager for a year, which could have provided a lot of additional income when I needed it due to the shortfalls in my business. It seemed to be a simple takeover. I was renting from someone who was selling the building(s) out of which my and his business ran, in which other tenants were based, and he was becoming a tenant there himself. He had a great concept that appeared to be doing really well at the time. He had a large space and slivered off many small, permanent booths that included everything a business might need; he rented for a low amount to more than thirteen different businesses. He branded it as *The Baker's Dozen* and promoted it like a mini market or mall but with diverse options for the consumer. The small businesses that rented from him ranged from artists and jewellery-makers to tattoo artists, baby needs, barbers, a record store, and a coffee shop, and he also staged events throughout the month, including movie nights, music nights, block parties, and even wedding receptions and social events.

He kept one building on the block, and with the proceeds from his sale, he planned to renovate that building into a cricket farm and possibly a restaurant later on. This major project needed his full attention, and he knew it. However, he didn't want to abandon the business he had started the year before, which on the surface was starting to gain some traction.

I had been renting from him for about eight months at the time, and we had had many conversations on such topics as real estate, employees, corporate taxes, contracts, future plans, the neighbourhood, and family. Because of my experience—with starting a business as the only employee, to having eighteen employees at one time, to being in the spot I was in, trying to rebuild my business and stave off bankruptcy—I was a good source of free advice for someone in his position and with his level of experience. He approached me with a good idea which favoured mostly him, but I was intrigued and gave his proposal some serious thought. He proposed that I manage his business, which meant collecting the rent, dealing with all the issues, creating a policy manual, helping promote the business, bringing in new business (renters or events), and managing the property. He would pay fixed costs such as rent, utilities, Internet, and insurance. He also expected that I would pay an agreed-upon fee every month that covered all his fixed-cost items and netted a small profit for him. This agreement would be in place for one year with options at the end. Those options would have included an extension or a purchase of the business, which would be based on a valuation of the business that my staff and I had built. We would build the business together, but the sale would profit him. The rent we were receiving from his sub-tenants at that time would barely cover the fee he wanted, although there were some open spots. Where we could make profit was with the possible events; however, events take a lot of work, and the renters got the event space included in their rent, limiting the event schedule.

I spoke with my manager about the possibilities, the ideas I had, and how I imagined the day-to-day logistics would work. From the costly lessons I had learned from my past, I did some due diligence and really debated and detailed the benefits and risks. In my free time and breaks, I went to all the current tenants and talked to them about what their future plans were, when their yearly lease was up, and what they thought could improve the space. After meeting with the current owner multiple times, talking to my accountant about tax implications, speaking to my lawyer about the liability risks, and considering the information shared by the tenants, we decided to pass.

He was making an offer that seemed to be the answer for the situation we were in at the time and could possibly generate an easy stream of income for us. But when we investigated more deeply and analyzed all aspects, we saw a great risk in exchange for the possibility of helping ourselves temporarily. For the owner, it was a good business move: if he could get someone to agree to his terms for a year, the deal would provide him with an income on top of his profit from the real estate deal and give him time to focus on his new venture. He would be getting his cake and eating it too. I couldn't blame him for trying; business is about serving your own best interest and making the best deals for those interests when you can.

In my experience from both sides of the table, people come to you looking to make a deal when they think they will get something out of that deal, or they try to make a deal out of desperation. Either way, they are looking to serve their best interests for the current situation or because of an opportunity that is available at that moment. Deals should be made with great thought and calculation. Luckily for us, we passed on this proposal; a couple of months later, the tenant occupancy dropped to only five from thirteen, leaving a gap between the income we would have received and that we would have been responsible to pay him, a dramatically negative shift. Although things had looked promising, with the opportunity to realize anywhere from one thousand dollars to four thousand dollars profit per month, we passed after due diligence and in consideration of our situation at the time. If we had agreed to this proposal, we would have been ruined because the negative cash flow would have been unbearable for us to sustain. The best deal I could have made in this situation was not to make a deal at all.

CHAPTER 10

GREED IS THE ROOT OF ALL EVIL

Wanting more financial security and personal wealth is not evil, nor is wanting to grow a business and make it highly profitable. However, the means by which you get there are vital to your reputation and long-term success. Putting money above everything else can become your downfall, and most times, greed will take you off an honest path. Many people have heard the term *stay the course*; but when people say that, what does it actually mean? As you become more successful, you become a magnet for people who want advice, money, or your time as an investment or criticism. You are never going to make everyone happy or make others successful. But greed can creep into your system as your success grows. When you have a solid plan with which you are comfortable, it should take a lot to convince you to take a chance on something that isn't in that plan. If you do consider deviating from your plan, keep in mind that if an opportunity sounds too good to be true, that is a red flag.

Such an opportunity came my way via a friend. He mentioned that I should meet with a man who had an investment that he believed would pay huge dividends. At the time, I was looking for another stream of income and thought I would hear this person out. I was suspicious, but intrigued; could something this easy just fall into my lap? To be sure and to cover my bases, when I went to meet him, I took my business lawyer with me. If the opportunity was above board, it could offer a great windfall.

The idea focused on the idea of a gifting club, presented by way of partial bits of tax law. We sat down with the presenter, not sharing real names upon his request, and readied ourselves for his spiel once his iPad was loaded. He started with what a gift is and insisted that gifts aren't taxable according to

Canada Revenue Agency law. He explained that because there was no trea-surer and participation was strictly voluntary, no laws would be broken. The presentation actually took the law out of context, providing bits to make the scheme seem genuine.

Basically, this was how the scheme worked. You make a payment of five thousand dollars to someone at a *birthday party*, and the person who is *birth-dayed* would collect five thousand dollars from eight people as gifts. You are at the lowest part of the pyramid at this point. You would then bring in two people to pay five thousand dollars at the next birthday party, which takes place when eight new people have joined. At that point, everyone would get bumped up a step on the pyramid. The progression would continue until you were at the top and got *birth-dayed*. Once you receive your forty thousand dollars at your *birthday*, you could choose to buy back in and start the process over in one pyramid or in multiple pyramids or leave completely.

The presenter told us that police officers, lawyers, doctors, accountants, and blue-collar workers were all participating. If you were looking to make easy money, it all looked like a great way to do so, but then danger signs began to appear. He said, without exception, that people had to abide by certain rules:

- Only code names were to be used and any email address we used had to be separate from our personal one.
- Only cash could be used, so there would be no paper trail. His reason was that some people were going through divorces and didn't want their activities to be found out by their ex-spouses.
- No advertising or turning this process into a business was allowed. This was to keep matters above board.
- The money had to be deposited bit by bit, so as not to raise questions from any authorities.

As he finished his presentation, he showed a page on his iPad that demon-strated they were a generous group, with a collage of charities of which they were a part of. This was the moment I became thoroughly suspicious because that's when one question rushed through my head: if there was no company, no treasurer, all cash payments, no commission, and no administration payment, where did all this charitable money come from?

We left, and not two steps out the door, my lawyer said, "Get as far away from this as fast as you can." He later sent me cases of people who had been arrested for this exact scam when it was perpetrated in other provinces, and he emphasized the possible penalty that I could face if I decided to get involved. What they had put in their presentation was directly from the Canada Revenue Agency website, but the information was not complete. Two of the many legal omissions they made were that a gift is only a gift if there is no expectations of further compensation and if there is no soliciting or recruitment, which were major pieces of their gifting model. A friend of mine, who was making over seven hundred thousand dollars per year at a secure, highly respected, and stable job, decided to get involved. He could not pass up the chance of making an extra thirty-five thousand dollars per year, tax-free, and he quickly started planning what he would do with all his new-found, easy money. Unfortunately for him, his employer found out and fired him. Others who he brought into the club, soon after he lost his job, started receiving calls from the police, who were investigating the matter. It turned out that the person who spearheaded the club was notorious for using everyone he could, and his scamming had been well known in London for years. This is a reminder of the old adage that, "If it's too good to be true, it probably is."

This may seem similar to a con, but I see it a bit differently. More than just losing some money to a con as a victim, here, you get a reward, and once you get that far, you're part of the entire act; you are now a perpetrator. In my friend's case, he lost a high-paying job with stocks, a pension, investments, and long-term security. Others were interviewed by the police to assist in an investigation against the very crime, although unwittingly, they had committed.

Greed creeps in slowly, like an infection, then, like an infection, it spreads until the host is severely sick or dies. It starts with a small gesture or favour for someone, and nothing happens initially. You carry on until a similar opportunity pops up, and you do it again, and again. You start to realize that the likelihood of getting caught is slim, and since the reward is substantial, you ignore your conscience and justify why and what you're doing. Little by little, you make increasingly more aggressive moves, which may not be illegal per se, but that will ultimately have a negative impact on your reputation if they are discovered.

When I started in the orthotic industry, I worked for a company that utilized a smart business promotion to increase their client base. If someone came in for the services the company offered, they would receive a credit. If a customer purchased orthotics, they received one credit for each pair of orthotics they purchased. If they purchased three pairs of compression socks, they received another credit and similar rewards for other purchases. The credit cost them ten dollars, which went towards the purchase of new footwear.

When I was hired, I was really nervous about this, but I quickly saw that no one seemed to care. When I started on my own, I did not offer any shoe deals that were tied to purchases of my products or services. I was in a busy doctor's office, renting space one day a week while working for the other company. I prided myself on doing a great job and finding the cause of a client's problem, even if my services could not help and they needed to be referred to other clinicians for initial treatment. But I wasn't making any money and had school and business debt looming over my head without being sure how I would pay it. I looked into many other similar businesses, and I found that most were doing some sort of similar promotion or they were already established in a perfect situation.

From a capitalist point of view, which allows people to be successful by offering similar products or services at greater value to the consumer, it shouldn't matter if someone offers footwear for a discount or even free. We did great assessments and gave the same advice and service as someone else but with added value when footwear was included at a discounted price. It was at great risk to obtain shoe accounts, as most cost up to five thousand dollars to be granted an account, and we had thirty shoe accounts. My personal feeling is that the other places that did not set up this many accounts weren't doing so because they didn't want to put money into said accounts. This practice was demonized and illustrated as a scheme, mostly because of some places abusing their clients extended benefit plan, and significantly increasing profits. Had those places not abused benefit plans, I do not believe adding value would have ever become an issue in the orthotic industry.

When I flipped to this business model, business went up ten-fold. In the Ottawa region, for example, business was incredible. People with benefits had their medical products paid for by their insurance company, and they got great shoes for ten dollars out of pocket. However, the management of companies that paid the insurance premium did not condone this model because of the subsequent increase in benefit claims. With pressure from the companies that paid the premiums, the insurance companies created a term called *claims abuse*, which branded everyone who participated in this model a criminal, and de-listed them, placing them on their banned provider's list.

There is a fine line between doing a straight promotion and committing fraud, and traditionally, when insurance companies investigated these clinics, they find other shady issues. You can't blame insurance companies for trying to keep costs down, even though they offer discounts and deals if you buy more than one plan from them.

I changed our business model, I recognized that the new insurance plans would eventually included the enactment of the *claims abuse* term within the plan. My initial feeling proved to be true; we actually had many customers come back year after year, even though we didn't offer the promotion anymore, because our product was sound, and they trusted the advice we gave them, especially when we referred them to another clinician before we created their device to be sure they had the best all-round care.

I shouldn't have had to change the business model because we weren't doing anything illegal or wrong; but since it was frowned upon, I made the decision to be cautious and transparent. I kept myself in check, didn't commit fraud, and made sure anything someone claimed on their benefit plan was something that they actually received with full service. Since changing our business model to stay aligned with the modified rules, I have been asked, and can see how difficult it can be to resist when people request a slight change in paperwork so they can maximize their benefits, getting more product while we received greater profit. This short gain could destroy long-term success.

Chapter 11

Be Honest During Adversity

This is a very easy thing to say but a very hard thing to do when speaking to or facing your creditors. Until or unless you have gone through difficult financial times, it may seem like a cliché, but it isn't. Most people are scared to admit that they are suffering through bad times or are failing, even temporarily. However, most people who are in or have been in business go through those moments at one time or another. Being upfront and honest with people usually does more in the end than trying to hide what is going on.

When everything seemed to be coming to an end for me, I owed many vendors and the Canada Revenue Agency a lot of money. At first, I didn't tell them what was happening, in hopes of turning it around before they needed to know the state of my affairs, but even then, I worked with them, answered their calls, replied to emails, and didn't make promises I couldn't keep. Nothing changes someone's opinion of you or makes them angrier than when you avoid them by all available means because you are hoping that the problem will just go away. Taking responsibility for your situation and the problem head on will gain you respect and understanding from even the toughest and most frugal of people.

It is very hard to threaten someone or walk over someone when that person could possibly lose everything yet is willing to take all the bad that comes with being down and out. With what do you threaten someone who is on the verge of losing everything? How can you not respect someone who is willing to work to pay back their debts when bankruptcy could save them? Going through this type of experience, I've learned a lot about bankruptcy and the difference between corporate and personal bankruptcy.

For most people, there are ways to get around the bad credit that will show up on future applications, and in the end, most credit companies' largest worry is about your asset/liability ratio, not a bad credit score. To me, declaring bankruptcy would put other businesses at risk because I couldn't live up to my commitments; while it might have taken me years to rebuild my business, I did not want it to be done at my vendor's or creditor's expense. At the end of the day, people want their money, and they don't want to deal with someone who is sneaky and devious—so they may show patience, but it will be short-lived if you lie to or avoid them.

Once I realized that I could not turn my financial situation around fast enough to satisfy all my creditors, I called the vendors and my Canada Revenue Agency representative and explained what had been done and what I was doing to get myself back on track. I clearly remember the feeling of that lump growing in my throat as I tried to explain what had occurred and my steps to recovery. I felt ashamed that I had put myself in this position by not making smarter moves to protect myself. For the most part, they all understood, and provided that I made an effort to pay what I could on my outstanding invoices when I could, they would wait.

Most people cringe at the thought of dealing with the CRA, especially when you owe them a lot of money; however, I found that the agent on my file was truly remarkable, both as a professional and a person. The CRA representative who oversaw my file took the time to hear me out and to explain the consequences if I failed to pay my HST debt; at the same time, she understood my situation. I was a father of two with no income but my wife's; was building a fourplex, and although was started before this happened, my credit was tied up; and my assets had been used as security, so I couldn't go get a loan to *stop the bleeding.* She understood that I had to keep my business going, and she wanted to see me get through this crisis without escalating my case into a legal matter.

I didn't know until she explained it thoroughly to me that failure to pay HST can land you in some serious trouble. When a business collects HST, that business is actually holding government funds in trust until the Canada Revenue Agency collects it from you. If you spend that money on other items, or use it for anything other than paying the CRA, you are technically misappropriating government funds, which is a crime that can carry a prison sentence—a worst-case scenario that rarely happens, but it can happen. The agents don't want to see this happen, but they have a job to do and to answer for. Also, agents hear every excuse imaginable, so lying will not work.

My agent set up a minimum payment schedule and dates to call her with updates, which I abided by to the letter. She could have just sent me right to the lawyers and possibly permanently ruined any future I might have, but she didn't. I also owed six vendors, two electricians, the bank, and money on lines of credit and credit cards. I didn't avoid any of their calls and I did not hide. Some could have threatened to send me to collections, which would have stained my credit and would have made it very problematic to get a loan to pay off these debts after my assets were free from being security on my construction project.

They all could have ignored my plea for time and understanding, but they didn't; they all tried to help where they could and to the extent that they could. I truly believe that they were as understanding as they were because I was as transparent as I possibly could be. Being honest and forthright and not avoiding awkward and shameful conversations, I put myself forward being as vulnerable as anyone could be; but I believed that they could see things were being turned around and that I was trying my best to remit the money my company owed them.

With the exception of HST, which is not resolved with bankruptcy protection—meaning you still need to pay it or face the consequences—the rest of the debt could have been erased by filing bankruptcy, which means I could have cleared up my HST, filed corporate bankruptcy, and used loopholes to restart under a different name and have a thriving business much more quickly. I didn't do that, although I was advised to, for the simple reason that I didn't want to have others experience stress, sleepless nights, and feelings of loss because of me. I would always know in the back of my mind that any success was at the cost of others and not truly deserved. I didn't want to sell my name. I followed my instincts, and because I was honest—and they could tell I didn't want to file for bankruptcy, even corporate bankruptcy—and was making the effort to pay them as fast as possible, they were willing to listen. I am not trying to shame someone who has had to file for bankruptcy, for some circumstances it is the only viable solution, the decision is not one I wish upon anyone. Also, the people I owed money realized that if I or my corporations were forced into bankruptcy, they would get only a small portion or nothing of what was owed. Through this experience, I found that the majority of people wanted to help where they could, and that in business, common sense and humanity can and do exist.

CHAPTER 12

TAKE THE SHOT

As a child growing up in a small Canadian village outside a small Canadian town, I had the same dream as most young Canadian boys did, which was to play in the National Hockey League. Anyone who gets into a big-league lineup, even if they don't get a second of playing time, has accomplished an amazing feat.

People who have had a career as a professional hockey player and kids dreaming of this have the common ability to ignore statistics and people constantly telling them that their dream is impossible. These negatives don't cripple their effort. Unfortunately, as in all walks of life, reality often sets in, and life dreams and priorities change. Some youngsters see the dream end at five or six years of age when they can't make a team above house league; some play AAA hockey until they reach the Bantam or Midget divisions before the dream dies because there aren't enough spots on teams past minor hockey; others, like me, get to play some junior hockey and try their hand at university, senior A, or semi-professional leagues; others do reach the professional hockey levels. With success comes reward, and big-league players are compensated very well. Ex-NHLers frequently state that they are lucky and owe everything they have in life, from money to family, to their success on the ice. This same sentiment applies to people who don't make a fortune, many met their wife while living in a foreign city or country, or they set themselves up for their lifetime in some way, as part of their participation in hockey.

I owe what I have to the game as well. Let me rephrase that: I owe what I learned and what I accomplished in the *real world* to what I learned from hockey. Because of hockey, I went to Pittsburgh for junior hockey to *test the waters*, to Europe to attend a semi-professional camp and to play for a short time in Scotland; I applied to Western University, after speaking to the head coach of the men's hockey team, where I lasted to the end, before they decided on their final roster; and I played senior AAA at a time when teams had rosters consisting of ex-professional players.

Because of my hockey experience, I still get invited to play a lot of recreational men's hockey. This last opportunity may be where it has benefited me most. It is where I made some valuable connections that have helped me in the past and still help me in business today. For all the hopeful players that didn't make it to the professional ranks but who pursued their dreams as far as they could, they learned a lot along the way. The higher level at which you play, usually, the more you learn about the importance of teamwork, hard work, loyalty, honesty, and adversity. Wayne Gretzky is the epitome of hockey greatness—hence the nickname, the Great One. Gretzky once stated, "You miss one hundred percent of the shots you don't take," a fitting quote from the greatest scorer and by far the greatest passer to ever play the game (Fleury et al.). So now, I take shots when I can—on the ice and off.

The willingness to take a chance happens most often when I am thinking of a new business. Usually when something in my life occurs, I try to see how that event could be turned into an idea or plan for business success, and I think there has to be an innovative way to make a profit.

When my daughter Stella was born, for instance, my wife and I were in the fortunate position of having benefits and both having disposable cash. My wife really wanted a home birth, meaning no interventions, which took me by surprise, and until I became educated about home births, I was a bit against the idea. This experience of home births and extended birthing services led me to start thinking about what has become the norm of hospital births and the financial aspects of pre- and postnatal care.

Birthing became a hospital norm performed by doctors in the 1900s to make more money and had little to do with the care of the patients. Birthing is a traumatic experience for both baby and mother; it takes weeks to recover from, and some of the earlier practices seem barbaric, to say the least, by today's standards.

We elicited the services of a midwife and discussed a birth plan that would require no interventions and would be completely natural, unless we were forced to the hospital for safety precautions for mother and/or baby. Our experience with a midwife was superlative, with prenatal meetings and three postnatal meetings that were very comforting and helpful. After both of our children's births, my wife was walking around, enjoying pizza and some beer as we celebrated the growth of our family, rather than being bedridden for multiple days.

Through my wife's pregnancy and after the birth, we used our benefits on physiotherapy for pelvic floor treatments, which is both to help prepare the mother for the birth and to help with a speedy and a more significant recovery. A physiotherapist, trained in pelvic floor exercises, represents a good investment because he or she can prepare my wife for the birth and help prevent future medical conditions and issues associated with birthing. We also used massage therapy, which can both relax the mother and help shift the baby to ease any pain that the mother may experience while carrying the child. We used chiropractic care, which helped to keep my wife operating at full capacity through proper alignment and provided her with some exercises to increase her comfort. We hired a doula, a trained professional who assists the mother and family with whatever their needs are during the birth and for the week following. I highly recommend having someone like a doula, who can see situations, from the outside, as a non-family member, who has the empathy and experience to relate to what is happening.

After our children were each six months old, we hired a sleep consultant. Mothers of young infants frequently are overwhelmed by pure exhaustion, emotional distress, and an inability to see an end to that cycle. When people are constantly tired, their health is affected as is their relationships with other members in the house, especially their spouse. After discussing our needs with the sleep consultant and following her advice, Stella went from being awake every three hours to sleeping twelve hours straight, a life-changing event for our family. We also met and followed the advice of a nutritionist to learn more about healthy eating both for prenatal and postnatal care. We would even have been willing to consult with a psychotherapist when things seemed to be spinning out of control, but the steps we would have to take to get this help covered by the benefits seemed overwhelming at that moment.

As we went through a great birth experience followed by the dramatic changes of a new baby and the attendant stressors that can push a relationship to the brink, I thought we were an isolated case, both bad parents and bad partners. Then, we started speaking with friends who had also had children, and we came to see that our experience was similar to theirs, which motivated my thinking even more; if the new-baby routine was like this for everyone and it was this hard, could there be a better way?

My entrepreneurial mindset kicked in, and I researched what the cost of a birth was at a hospital, where you might stay one night or possibly two nights before being sent home to face those challenges on your own. Only people with disposable income and benefits could access most of the above-mentioned services, which excludes a large portion of the population and often the ones that need the most help. After I started researching the different services and their costs and met with professionals in those fields, all the while remembering how my wife handled both her pregnancies and deliveries, a few things became clearer:

- Women are resilient and don't always need interventions to give birth.
- All professionals repeat that a strong start to a child's life is key to future success.
- Expectant parents, including me, can be uneducated and ill-prepared.
- The cost at hospitals is far more than the cost of using a midwife.
- Many parents simply accept what doctors and TV have told them about birthing.

I started a business plan for a birth centre that included all the services mentioned for the mother, baby, and family and would take birthing out of the hospitals, freeing up needed beds within the hospital. It would create tens of millions of dollars in tax revenue by growing the customer base for all the service providers. The plan would give all the professionals who provide the services and the OBGYN a significant raise because the business model would be laid out so the doctors involved would eventually take over the fully equipped birth centres, which would become their headquarters. Many people assume that socialized medicine means doctors are employees of the government, but doctors are actually self-employed corporations.

Financially speaking, the proposed birth centre saves the province fifteen to twenty-five percent on the cost of a birth at the time of the birth. This proved to be a difficult number to estimate because of how our system works, so I followed the advice of a retired MP and used the costs at bordering

American state hospitals to estimate costs in Canadian hospitals. With the United States still utilizing a private system, which itemizes everything, this became a very useful tool in my analysis.

I wanted my plan to avoid political party lines, so all politicians could agree that this would be a plan that would keep everyone in mind. To be a positive move for all political parties, the plan needed to be fiscally responsible, socially responsible, medically responsible, and community-oriented, and it would need to help all classes of families to deal with pregnancy right through and up to the end of the first year of the baby's life. Giving the mothers and families support physically and emotionally and helping answer questions they may not even know to ask, the goal was to give all babies the best foundation possible while at the same time, saving taxpayers money and providing a service for members of every socio-economic sector. I also wanted the plan to benefit the community, and I believed that with the help of the services mentioned—especially the psychotherapy, more children would have parents in less-stressed situations, which would, in turn, help keep families together.

This sounds logical and positive on paper; however, it could only work if the provincial government would first agree to do a pilot project, with someone like me to quantify the business results. So when I say, "I'm taking a shot," I really mean just that. I would have to gain access to the health minister of Ontario after submitting a very persuasive written plan for that minister's team to review. I would then have to convince that office to move forward, so my plan would reach the Premier's desk. It would have to impress them enough that they would offer to meet with me. If that happened, I would have to make a pitch that would grant approval to run this program in London, where I could monitor it and provide the government with all the information this project accumilated. The chances of these "ifs" becoming "whens" is slim to nil. However, thinking something will never happen or that the status quo is set in stone will make these assumptions truths.

In high school, I had a gym teacher who adored a local hockey player and referenced him in all his classes. Said player was accomplished; he played junior B at fifteen, led his team, and maybe even the league, in scoring at sixteen, he went on to the Ontario Hockey League, played on the World Junior Team, winning gold and scoring the team's last three big goals. He was drafted sixth overall in the NHL entry draft, made his NHL debut at nineteen, and later won The Stanley Cup.

In class one day, the teacher made a comment I still remember. He said that the local hockey player would "go on to make more money in one year than you will in a lifetime." I don't believe he was saying this to insult me, he simply admired and adored that player. I've realized that that was a great indirect teaching moment for me. Had I believed that I was from a small town and had limited options, as many do in small towns, I would have never tried my hand in Pittsburgh, Europe, or even gone to university. Because I made those attempts to continue to play hockey, I received a university degree, have a postgraduate designation, and became an entrepreneur, which led me to a chance meeting with the woman who is now my wife and the mother of our two children.

Nothing has to be set in stone. You can shoot for the stars if you choose to, unless you believe the former is true. Although the odds are greatly stacked against many of us, we cannot make a significant difference if we do not try to make what seems impossible a reality. I am willing to do the work; I am willing to take a chance; I will try to follow Wayne Gretzky's advice to score by taking a shot.

CHAPTER 13

OVERSIGHT OVERKILL

You look at your business, see how far it has come, and feel like you deserve some time to enjoy what you've built. You step back and enjoy the good life; you trust your employees are doing their jobs well; you let little things slide. But the little thing, compounded by many little things, can keep growing until you're broke.

Sitting down once or twice a week to go over everything, from top to bottom, may seem like micromanaging, but unless you're a massive company with managers who do that for you and report back to you, someone with authority needs to know what is happening on every front of the business. This also sends a strong message to staff and customers that you are on top of everything. Such a policy helps avoid catastrophic errors involving customers and prevents negligence on the part of staff. This behaviour can be implemented at any time. If you have a partner and push for this type of oversight and that person tries to avoid that conversation, consider this avoidance as a big red flag.

When I had a partner and we had six locations across Ontario and Quebec, we made a gentleman's agreement that he would handle the business side, and I would handle the clinical side. I noticed right from the start that bills were not being entered into our accounting software and clients weren't being called to inform them that their products were ready. I originally presumed that these lapses were due to his taking on a new role and job and that he simply needed time to adjust and become proficient, so I let it slide.

After a couple of years of expansion, I couldn't dismiss the feeling that we should have been realizing more profit than we were. I inquired but got vague answers that were more deflection than information. Finally, I forced a meeting with our accounting firm, a company that my partner used in the Ottawa region, that hadn't ever met me, and that might not even have known about me. I came prepared with questions to have answered directly by the accountant, with no room for misinterpretations or for anything lost in translation.

I quickly realized that our business was not being run correctly. My partner had hired so many people that he didn't have to work, and he had incurred unjustifiable expenses—hiring personal contacts for jobs in areas that were already overemployed, putting his entire household's cellphones on the company plan, claiming mileage for his travel, but also putting his car lease through the business, and not following up with people to collect and pay for their products. At one point, we had one hundred pairs of orthotics sitting on shelves, just waiting to be picked up. These had cost us ninety-five dollars to have made, but we charged five hundred dollars per pair to cover time, knowledge, and service. Added to this problem were the unsold stock of shoes, compression socks, and other products, which amounted to approximately eighty thousand dollars. My partner didn't follow any suggested procedures or policies and let the staff do as they pleased, so they didn't care or didn't realize the amount of potential income that was just sitting there. Why would they?

At that point, I made changes, but most of them were reversed after I left. Later, as the same issues arose, I discovered that my partner had taken a thirty-thousand-dollar dividend that I had never received, and he was allowing a staff member with whom he had a personal relationship to take paid days off, to arrive late and to depart early, but she was being paid for the entire day. He was also dining out personally and writing the dinners off as a company expense, and he was claiming personal costs as company expenses. The final straw was a home renovation in excess of fifty thousand dollars that was paid for by the company.

Had I been meticulous over every detail from the start and set meetings every time I was there, meaning every three weeks at first, I would have known what was not done from the last time I was there, and I could have made a plan that he needed to live up to for when I returned. With that type of oversight, I would have caught all this far sooner. Further, it would have sent a stern message to employees, as they joined our company, that we believed in following policies to the letter, with everyone required to do their jobs properly in the established structure.

Most importantly, it would have sent a message to my business partner that I knew what was happening at all times. This action would have reduced some of the issues I went through with him, although it wouldn't have resolved all of them. When you stop a con artist from doing one thing a certain way, he or she will look for another path to get where they want to go; the more doors you close, the more ways he or she will try, until all avenues are exhausted. Only at that point, in my experience, will that person give up trying or want out.

No matter how good a situation is for them, this kind of manipulator thinks they can get more with a scheme. Had I understood the psychology of a con artist better, I would have known long before I did with whom I was dealing and what his end goals were. He would have known much sooner that he couldn't get away with not working or stealing from the company. This would have saved us hundreds of thousands of dollars in profits, tens of thousands of dollars in personal tax, and given us a chance to sell a company with much more value. It would also have given me the peace of mind of being able to trust the people around me or the option of getting away from them. If you're on the top, you should know everything that is happening, for no other reason than that everything will eventually become your problem if you don't take care of trouble early.

Extensive oversight is even more important if you are named as a director of the company. All business operations, tax deductions, HST remittance, and company debt could fall on your lap if you decide to, or agree to become a director of the company. The title sounds prestigious, but there are vast responsibilities that are linked to that role and that could ruin you if you are unaware of the rights and responsibilities of such role.

CHAPTER 14

RANDOM SENSE

Just a paycheque: I once worked at a wonderful restaurant and really loved the owner, and I still respect him. I remember we had a staff meeting, a necessary routine exercise to make sure that things that had to be addressed were. He had just become the owner, previously having been the manager. He was adjusting to the clean-up he had to take on from the previous owner, and he was learning the difference between being a manager and being an owner, which I'm sure was very stressful.

During the meeting, he became passionate about how he expected his staff to be there for more than just a paycheque and to go the extra mile. This has stuck with me since for the simple reason that the majority of the jobs that people do are only for the paycheque. It is not the employees' responsibility to make your business an employee-friendly place to work and to inspire themselves to go that extra mile: it's yours as the owner. Employees are there to be paid, but the business is your livelihood, and if done properly, it will be there after many employees have come and gone. Inspire your staff by being a responsible businessperson and human. If you're good to them, most will return the respect they feel. If others are just there for a paycheque, provided they do their job, why does it matter? If you know that, you can manage accordingly.

Be a leader: Give the business and, in turn, the employees direction. Oversee the work they are doing and give constructive feedback; be a strong, confident figure that they can look up to. Be open to ideas, but be in charge; instill your staff's faith in you. They should know and believe that when push comes to shove, you're there for them.

Educate: I have read that experience is what we call our mistakes. Let staff make mistakes, but teach and guide them to reduce future mistakes. I have one employee who graduated from the same university programs I did and has the same credentials I do. He excels at his job, and over the years, he has come to learn about the industry, my mistakes, and what I learned from those errors. Seeing how little he knew about business those many years ago illustrates how little I knew when I started. We all need to learn; keeping people ignorant will hurt you more than it does them. If you teach them so much that they go on their own, so be it; you have done your job.

Work: The worst thing one can do is to become complacent in business and fail to work hard. My ex-business partner illustrated this perfectly. He looked at being an owner as meaning you didn't need to work, and he delegated everything. This strategy caused over-staffing. One staff member would tell him they needed help, and because he didn't know the job, he would hire more people to do jobs that one person should have been able to do. When the help was needed, he should have stepped in himself and worked through the situation. Staff recognized his attitude, and they became lazy too.

Be accountable: Nothing frustrates employees more and diminishes their respect for their employer more than a boss who passes the buck. Admit your mistakes and allow staff to do the same. Learning from mistakes and being accountable will take the business much farther than side-stepping blame. If you accept blame and hold yourself accountable, most of your staff will as well.

Allocate responsibility: If you have to babysit your employees, you've hired the wrong people for the job. At one restaurant where I worked during university, the manager wouldn't give me closing responsibility, which was the shift that made the most money. He didn't like me and thought I was incapable of following a checklist. At this point in my life, I had been a manager in that industry, was in a post-graduate program, ran my own business, owned a home, and worked another job part-time.

This situation started to bother me, negatively affecting my performance and the effort I put in. I felt unappreciated and believed that I was there only as a *filler* and not as someone the restaurant would rely on. Because of this perception, I came in unprepared to work, not always as clean-shaven as I could have been, and sometimes with wrinkled clothes. I did the bare minimum. I treated the job as I felt I was being treated, while prior to this manager taking over, I did all that was asked of me and more. One person's attitude changed all that for the worse.

Be consistent: Stick by your policies; don't change them on a whim, based on who violated the policy. Showing consistency will add accountability and faith in you as an employer; not doing so will have the opposite effect.

I was hired at one company where I was told that part-time people might get better shifts because the company believed in seniority and rewarded people who had been with them for years. I liked that, even though, at the time, part-time people could make more money than I could as full-time. I was between my undergraduate and postgraduate program then. When I started my postgraduate program, I had moved to the top end of seniority, and thought it was going to be great to continue to make full-time money while in school. However, that September, the manager who did the scheduling made a change. *Now* the policy was based on availability. So, although I was first or second in line, after all the employee changes, I was now back to doing the weaker shifts because I was part-time and not as available. People who had just been hired were getting the best shifts and making more money than I was. This also negatively affected my performance.

Find your niche: Expect plenty of competition. I have moved into a business model of volume with low price points on manufacturing and services, but mostly I have moved into bringing new products to market or building on those already in place. Competing with established and recognized businesses that offer exactly the same products and services may end successfully, but this model is formidable unless you have something different to offer.

The difference doesn't have to be huge, but there has to be an individual *something*. A friend of mine owns an insurance brokerage that offers a life insurance policy that is designed especially for businesses, a worthwhile product if you can afford the premium. This distinguishes his company as subtly different from the rest, but it is different enough to drive a successful business.

Compete in your space: Knowing your strengths so you can build on them and recognizing a losing battle are both crucial perspectives. A retired NHL hockey player who lives in London had a great career: Memorial Cup champion, World Junior Gold Medalist, thirty-second overall draft pick, two Stanley Cups, and contracts worth north of sixty million dollars by his retirement in his thirties. In his final season in the OHL, he tallied fifty-seven goals and 130 points in fifty-nine games for the London Knights—impressive by all accounts. But the NHL success might never have happened if he hadn't made one huge realization, one that many players in similar situations don't make and who don't have as successful NHL careers as he did, or an NHL career at all.

When this hockey player attended the Chicago Blackhawks training camp as a centre, there were two other talented players who were also slated to play centre—Patrick Kane and Jonathan Toews. This man took stock and realized that to make the cut and to be an impactful player for that team, he needed to change from a top point producer to a third-line centre, something he did very well. He didn't bother competing with the two players who were projected as the future of the franchise; instead, he competed in his own space. He went from being unlikely to make the team to being the top candidate in the role he took on. Success is not always measured by the people at the top and should be considered in your own space and terms.

Everything becomes a job: The more success you achieve, the more responsibility you take on and the more work you need to do. You may be able to afford more employees to whom you can delegate tasks, but your workload will increase through just the acts of organizing and communicating with your staff.

Many people believe that the people in professional sports, the ones who make it to the big leagues, live a life of primarily fun and notoriety. In reality, the higher you rise, the less time you can take off. In the off-season, training is essential; you must go to the gym to work as hard as your body will allow, while still maintaining proper diet and rest. During the playing season, practice, diet, and rest become even more essential for you to be at your best for practices and especially for every game. Add marketing to the schedule, as well as the endless rounds of public relations—meeting fans and participating in team functions within the community, charity work, constant requests to spend your free days and weekends at golf tournaments or other events where you need to be cordial, friendly, and outgoing. You must reveal enough of yourself that the people who have paid handsomely to be there feel compensated, but at the same time, you cannot violate the league and team standards in your contract. There is the pressure to perform perfectly in every game that needs to be balanced against the needs of friends and family. An outsider sees glamour, but for these athletes, it is a full-time job, and the higher the profile of that athlete, the higher the expectations. They face frustration, hard work, alienation, and stress on a daily basis. Like these athletes, you are your business twenty-four seven.

Be humbly competitive: Success is always the goal, and sometimes success means you beat someone else. You may outbid them, take their market share, or innovate in a way that makes them obsolete.

Being competitive drives me; it motivates me in tough times and keeps me focused during the good times. No matter how much you want something or how much you *win*, being humble is of the utmost importance. If you become wildly successful, being humble will keep you in touch with your industry, your competitors, and, most importantly, with friends and family. No one likes having someone else's success flashed in their face, nor does anyone want to feel belittled or diminished. You never know who will become an ally or potential partner down the road, and your reputation will leave an impression on them even if you have yet to meet. Further, success is not always permanent, and you never know what could tip the scales to a downfall. People routinely help rebuild businesses and lives, but they are more likely to help you if you've always been a decent, modest person.

CHAPTER 15

CORRECTED

When a person finds themselves in a desperate position and hopes something will go their way to help fix the problem, but that moment never comes, what does that person ultimately do?

In my case, I tried any and every solution I could imagine, but in the end, the solution came down to tough decisions and hard work. I needed to free up cash, which meant selling assets with any value for what I could get.

My first investment was a small Ontario cottage that was close to downtown London, in a neighbourhood known as Old North, which I had purchased in 2012. Prior to purchasing this building, I had been paying rent to a doctor for a small room in his medical building. My rent was fifteen percent of my revenue, so as I did better, the rent increased. At times, I was paying four thousand dollars or more in rent to the doctor, and another thousand dollars a month for rent on my apartment, plus utilities. By purchasing this building in Old North, I had been able to cut costs considerably by moving my office into the front half of the building and living in the back half. Now the total cost for my business and personal space was a total of two thousand dollars a month, which included property tax and the utilities, with all other costs approximately the same as at my old apartment.

A great location for business and/or a rental property, the building was on a corner lot close to downtown with a bus stop on the corner. My long-term plan was to build up and turn it into a triplex with two, two-bedroom apartments and a one-bedroom apartment. Because I owed such a small amount on my mortgage, I would be increasing the rental income and value of the building, instantly increasing the equity to the hundreds of thousands. I loved that building, and it had significant sentimental value to me; unfortunately,

I had to sell it and take the equity I had to settle up with as many creditors as possible. My plan to renovate that site and have a property worth between nine hundred thousand and a million dollars at the time of retirement was now a lost dream. By selling this investment, however, I was able to partially pay what I owed to the private lenders for the fourplex that we had built the previous year and on which I still owed some creditors.

The fourplex I built was sold at fair market value, which turned out to be short of the amount I needed to pay everyone. I still owed over two hundred thousand dollars to creditors. Although I learned a lot through this experience that will hopefully serve me well in the future, by choosing to pursue this project, I added extreme financial and emotional stress to my family's life. I had also rolled the one hundred thousand dollars of personal tax into this project. The total cost after everything if we hadn't done this project was comparable within the thousands of dollars, but minus the stress. The emotional and marital stress I added isn't possible to quantify. Further, we may need to refinance a small amount on our marital home to finish paying all my personal and business debts from these events. We will have to be extremely frugal for the next few years, but we will put any surplus money onto our home mortgage to reduce it to the amount it would have been before this all happened, if we need to refinance.

We built the fourplex knowing that the rental rates would more than cover the expected mortgage; with this second property, we could have added the value of the fourplex and the rental income to our retirement plan. By the time of retirement, we would have a property worth around two million dollars, totalling over three million dollars, if not more, in real estate holdings, with all mortgage free, we would have had the option of collecting the surplus rent as a pension or sold the properties to enjoy the gains we accumulated.

As I moved to advance my business forward and as my debts were still being settled, I followed the advice I now advocate. When looking into a new space to lease from a prospective landlord, I planned to renovate the unit and sub-lease the additional offices I was installing. Instead of just going ahead and doing so, I spoke with my accountant, inquiring about any tax implications of sub-leasing. I sent the proposed lease to my lawyer for review, and I negotiated with the landlord, saving three month's rent and a few hundred dollars per month. I also received quotes for all renovation costs before agreeing to the terms of the lease for that building. This space allowed for multiple practitioners (up to six in additional to myself) to sublease my space; one of the negotiations I added to the lease—to bring my rent down to much lower than it was before—was for an additional space that would house my manufacturing and retail portion in the same space, which would cut down on labour and the need for additional staff as we grew as I needed to rent a second location just for manufacturing.

I also participated in the University of Waterloo's co-op placement program, which aims at helping small businesses with social media campaigns. I was reimbursed seventy-five percent of the student's wages, and got a thirty-five percent write-off for their wages. This program was helpful in securing more referrals via social media. Social media is important, but its use was a daunting task for me having little experience in the space. Having a young individual who is educated and experienced available to assist in a space they understand better than I do was beneficial to my business. It enabled me to maximize the ratio of ad costs to referrals from social media; understand the analytics; and learn the most efficient and effective editing tools for marketing and posts in the social sphere.

We also had the co-op student make an instruction manual that clearly illustrated her methods for when her term was completed. This manual gave us something we could refer to after she had departed. To further increase referrals for assessments, I joined a doctor's concierge service. Partnering with them funnelled possible clients my way by linking me to other members of his concierge service and promoting my services directly to the other members and their staff. By implementing these different strategies, my business turned around and slowly returned to a profitable position.

I also have a new product, which is scalable worldwide, about to enter the market. I invented an outsole that has a removable heel, which has intrigued some surgeons and physiotherapists with its huge potential as a post-surgical footwear device that can assist the recovery of patients with total hip or knee replacements. When a patient receives a total hip replacement, and in some cases, total knee replacement, up to fifty percent start their recovery with a temporary leg-length discrepancy, which slowly lengthens back to normal or nearly normal by the end of their physical rehabilitation. However, with a significantly shorter leg, at times up to two centimetres shorter, the patient walks with a limp because their centre of gravity has been displaced and their gait is disrupted and unnatural. The other, and more important aspect, is that the shorter leg causes anterior adduction (which causes the leg to move towards the midline of the body) and internal rotation; these forces will pull on the new hip joint when the patient puts weight on it, which, in turn, can cause dislocation, which forces a revision surgery. Revision surgery is a more difficult and costly surgery than the initial operation because surgeons need to correct the replacement. To maximize recovery, physiotherapists get patients up and walking right after surgery, within four hours for some. My outsole can help correct this potentially damaging leg-length difference. The Ontario government allocates a block sum of money to be used for the surgery and recovery, and if we can prove a benefit to introducing the outsole after replacement surgery, we may be able to include a pair in those block payments.

This idea was born from experience in my field as a pedorthist. I used to meet with clients a few days prior to their surgery to cut off the outsole of their shoe. Then I would wait until we heard what the leg-length difference was, add material to make up the difference, and return the shoe to the client. As the leg would lengthen, we would repeat the process as many times as needed until the patient achieved a final leg length upon the conclusion of recovery. By the end of the process, the client had a damaged shoe that they couldn't use, had paid me for my time for every adjustment, and still had to purchase new footwear. I had an idea, but could I make it functional and safe to use? If I could design an outsole device that had removable heels, this would solve the problem and provide a tool for physiotherapists to use during recovery. So I did.

With the help of a 3-D printing company which already made custom sandals, I designed an outsole for a sandal, with plans for a shoeline, that has a removable heel, so the patient can correct the difference by exchanging a neutral heel height of the outsole to the heel height with the desired correction for the shorter leg. A patient can exchange the heels as many times as needed. At the end of the process, the patient has a quality footwear with a more efficient correction in heights that either they or their physiotherapist can change. This saves the person having to book an appointment to see someone like me, and it means much less financial burden by the end of the recovery process.

These outsole do not exist at the moment, and once proven to work, allows rehabilitation centres to add another tool to their treatment plan, increase revenue, and build reputation; hospitals could even increase their revenue by selling the device themselves, once they are incorporated into footwear safely. With more than sixty thousand hip replacement and seventy thousand knee replacement surgeries performed in Canada annually, the customer source is plentiful and is constantly being renewed. Currently, we are conducting a study at University Hospital here in London, ON, on the theory of the outsoles, which I believe will prove they:

- Increase patient's comfort during gait.
- Decrease recovery time.
- Increase positive recovery results.
- Decrease revision surgeries due to dislocation.
- Maintain a proper gait from the first step after surgery until recovery is complete.

If a patient walks with a limp, even if they have no pain, their brain can determine that the limp is their correct or normal gait pattern; it will force that gait pattern onto them, leaving them with a permanent limp, which can have further complications throughout the kinetic chain.

Through a friend who was finishing his fellowship as an orthopedic surgeon at Toronto Western Hospital, I was able to present the outsole to the surgical team, describing how it worked and having them try it on themselves. I was informed on a Monday at lunch that they could get me in to present the very next day at seven in the morning. So, I arranged for childcare, quickly organized my wife's professional obligations and made accommodations for that night in Toronto, and polished my presentation to the standard to which surgeons are accustomed.

The currency to present was eleven McDonald's breakfast combos for the doctors and residents who would attend the morning presentation, so my plan was to awaken at five in the morning, get ready and out of the Airbnb within the hour, find parking near the hospital, get to the McDonald's across from the hospital, and make it into the room and set up with time to spare.

My alarm went off; I popped out of bed, groomed myself, and quickly ate breakfast as planned. I texted my friend to see how things were looking, but the texts that usually appear in a blue text box were now sitting in a green text box.

I left my Airbnb as instructed, leaving the keys where the confirmation reservation directed, and stepped into the elevator. Unfortunately, you needed the key fob for the elevator to work, so I was stuck. Luckily, after a few minutes, another tenant, also up early and heading to the exercise facility, got into the elevator. He was kind enough to give me instructions on how to get out of the building. I was a little delayed but still on my way. I stopped at McDonald's, put my order in, and continued trying to get a text response from my friend.

At twenty minutes to seven, I had waited thirty minutes and still had no food in hand, and I had no response from my friend, so my anxiety was kicking into overdrive. I tried calling my friend, but the automatic response that answered said that the phone number was not assigned. I finally received my food and rushed over to the hospital. I went through the revolving doors and directly over to information. There I requested that they contact the appropriate doctor, but they weren't sure how to do that. At that moment, I received a text from a number I didn't recognize. It was my friend, who had changed his number over the weekend. We met in the lobby, and he walked me to the room in which I would be presenting.

We walked in at five minutes past seven to an empty room. I was a bit relieved to have time to set up my computer and get prepared to present. In my attempt to do so, the A/V equipment proved not to be working, meaning that I would have very little to present. The gem of the entire presentation was my video of a client suffering from a leg-length discrepancy, but the A/V never got sorted out, so, I tried to demonstrate everything from my laptop and my prototype.

I had only ten minutes allotted to me at the beginning of the class, and everyone, including the surgeon who was teaching the class, was late. I was cut off about five minutes into the presentation and had to sit with the resident surgeons through their hour-long knee arthroplasty class. I had spent approximately five hundred dollars at this point to get there and present, and the planned presentation was barely and only partially seen.

After class, my friend and I moved the leftover McDonald's breakfasts into the doctors' lunchroom, and he asked me to text him in about an hour, so we could get the lunch presentation sorted out. I put on a confident front, but inside I felt deflated. I left the hospital and moved my car, contemplating what I should do. I just wanted to go home; the thought of waiting for the next three hours to probably get a similar response was very unappealing. My friend contacted me and said that pizza and pop would do for lunch. There was a pizza place in the hospital, so I didn't have to stray far to get what they wanted. He then texted, "Do you think it is worth it to stay?" My anxiety was saying, "No," but my gut and brain were saying, "You're here; just do it." So, I responded positively and stayed.

I walked the pizza up to the lunchroom and sat on a chair just outside. A few people who likely felt obligated to talk to me for the free lunch asked some questions and were very polite and complimented the product before they went back to work. Then, in an instant, an older surgeon came to see it, telling me he only had a few minutes to talk, so I got right into it. My pitch started, "These outsoles have a removable heel for people with leg-length discrepancies, especially after hip replacement surgery. The theory is they will quicken the rate of recovery and garner better and lasting results for recovery." I was about thirty seconds into my pitch when he asked me how they worked, so I quickly showed him. His reaction was exactly what I needed, "This is brilliant. This doesn't exist?" Before I could answer his question, the surgeon who had previously cut me off to go ahead with teaching said over my shoulder, "This is what I was telling you about this morning." They took my card and referred me to someone to set up another luncheon in a few weeks to discuss how to get the sandals into their hospitals.

This hospital is tied in with the University Health Network and is connected to four hospitals that perform thousands of hip and knee replacement surgeries per year. I left happy, validated, and excited. Had I not gone back for lunch but simply left, feeling depressed and deflated, none of this would be possible. I constantly tell my staff that you need to treat everyone you see with the utmost professionalism and respect because you never know who will be that one person who becomes your tipping point. I visited the hospital a few weeks later and did what was essentially a repeat of the first lunch presentation. However, this time, a few people from other departments came to meet me and see the product. One was the coordinator of the physiotherapy clinic in the hospital. We exchanged cards and emails later that week and planned to meet with more administrators to work out pricing and logistics for the product. Unfortunately, this we just prior to the Covid-19 pandemic so nothing materialised.. With the study at University Hospital being conducted I'm in a better position now than I was then because the paper will be published by surgeons to support my theory.

I have always tried to keep up with the trends in our industry, including health insurance changes to customer benefit plans and their constantly changing standards. Reviewing our volume, since it was declining, and speaking with whomever I could in the insurance industry, I learned that insurance companies were changing policies and monitoring places that exceeded a certain threshold of revenue. These new policies derived from past cases of fraud that they found in clinics that had high levels of revenue. I believe that this is a great opportunity to showcase our services because we know that we conduct business ethically.

We also spoke with our current business associates, asking how many referrals they sent our way per month. It turned out that for every ten referrals that they sent, only one or two, in a good month, were actually making an appointment with us. After some deliberation, an option that I had not thought of before occurred to me. We added a service to our business model that is bringing in a stream of patients and will continue to increase income over the following years. We have found that if we go into clinics for a fair and reasonable price, other clinics can profit from our work, and we can still make money ourselves. It is far easier to have the therapist that the client trusts book an appointment right there on the spot for orthotics and be serviced at their clinic than to send the client off with a referral on which most clients don't follow through. We need to double the volume for the same revenue, and of course, travel costs will be incurred, but we can realize more than twenty times the referral sources that will actually use the service and product. This move is not different from what many other pedorthists do, but from the information from clinics with which we are dealing, the pricing is.

Because we have a fully functional lab to make the orthotics traditionally, either CNC-milled or 3-D printed, we can charge the clinic an enticing price. The clinics we visit make a healthy profit from our service, instead of losing that revenue by sending their clients off with a referral. We exponentially increase our revenue while the clinic offers a quality service with licensed clinicians that they didn't have access to before, keeping them ahead of the coming changes by insurance companies concerning who is qualified to assess, manufacture, and dispense orthotics.

Furthermore, the pricing protects me from being undercut. Most clinicians do not have access to a fully functional lab or the manpower to handle this part of the work. If they were to offer a lower price and had to pay a lab to make their orthotics, after travel, they would make such a small profit that the effort wouldn't be worth their time. Further, if a clinic, even a large clinic with multiple locations, wanted to hire a full-time person for that role, they would need a volume that most would never reach. They would also have to deal with payroll taxes, vacation requests, sick days, and all the other issues that come with an employee. With the three methods of production that we employ to produce orthotics, we are manufacturing for other clinicians such as pedorthists, chiropodists, podiatrists and chiropractors. Because of technology, we can do a high volume without adding staff and increase our profit margins. We have also altered how we purchase inventory and sell merchandise, increasing our profit margins on those products. I am confident it won't take long until my business has regained its former prosperity and accomplishments.

In the midst of all this, and as we started offering our on-site service at many new clinics and had a month's appointments set up, both at our clinics and others, we prepared for the first significantly profitable month in two years. However, in our type of business, you do the work, invoice at the end of that month, and clients have another month to pay their invoice. This is standard business practice, but at the same time, I needed to pay my bills for two more months to start making profit. A relative generously helped me out, in spite of him being severely taken advantage of in the past, without a contract of any sort. How can I not succeed when I have people like him in my life who have so much faith in me? I have no room for failure.

I was set to move forward full force, then the COVID-19 pandemic hit. It completely shut all the clinics to which we provide manufacturing and services to and ourselves down. I felt terrible—absolutely deflated and depressed. I had spent twenty months fighting to stay afloat by paying the

Canada Revenue Agency, vendors, other professional services and creditors, maintaining a good reputation within my industry, and maintaining the professional connections I had made. I also had to cope with the alarming knowledge that my patent had to be filed within months to maintain the worldwide rights to my sandals, and this would cost twenty-three thousand dollars. And I was back to a position of limited revenue. I had to temporarily lay off all my staff and cut every cost I was able to without completely sinking my business.

I applied for all assistance that was available from the government and hoped I still had a business when the pandemic ended. I really felt as if no matter what I did, something greater than me and beyond my control was trying to hammer that final nail into my coffin. I had followed the rules and stayed within the requirements that the government laid out, and I qualified for the small business loan and the wage subsidy. I needed cash flow, but because of my past couple of years of net negative profit, no bank would lend me anything to keep going, so I had to maximize my assistance. Then, more bad news. Many clinics that we provided services to did not qualify for the pandemic assistance and were unsure if they could remain in business. That meant that they would not be paying their outstanding invoices to my business until assistance arrived, if it ever did.

Everything has a way of correcting itself, as we see when real estate prices soar, then plateau, and even plummet at times. The people buying at the end of the bubble are stuck with a high mortgage rate: they are often unable to get what they need back if they have to sell within the first five years, and they can only hope they make it to when the next bubble hits. The stock market goes in cycles of boom and bust, and during the last eleven years, it was referred to as a bull market, meaning a correction is long over due.

In business, if you ever think you have everything figured out, don't learn from your mistakes fast enough, or let emotions or innocence cloud your judgement, a negative result will surely occur. I came from a lower middle-class family and worked my way up, but when I got to a position of wealth, I thought I was ready to take on larger projects. I spread myself thin and took on tasks that I wasn't yet prepared for, education or experience-wise, and I did not follow all the advice I have shared in this book. I put my family in a dire position. Mentors advised me that I was making the right moves, and

I started to think that disaster could never happen to me, pushed aside the pessimistic counter advice, and heard only what I wanted to hear, making it impossible for me to come to a logical fully-informed decision. In short, life corrected me. "Plan for the best; prepare for the worst" remain words to live by in life and business.

After everything I have been through and all I have lost due to poor business judgment, arrogance, and unrealistic, wishful thinking, I finally see a silver lining. It has been an expensive education, but had I not made these colossal mistakes and learned some very valuable lessons, had everything worked out as planned, I would have gone on doing business in that same manner. Imagine how much more I could have lost farther down the line with more assets and cash at stake? I have licked my wounds, learned my lessons, and moved on. Hopefully, I have emerged stronger than before as I continue to recover from my losses. I am now planning a profitable and secure future, so I can one day, with my family by my side, look back at this as a bump in the road, not a permanent detour. Destruction leads to a very rough road, but it also inspires creation. Most importantly to me, I can use this time to illustrate to my children that, through all this turmoil and how severely I was corrected, I never sold my name.

Resources

Allchin, Douglas. "Science Con-Artist." The American Biology Teacher, University of California Press, 2012, https://online.ucpress.edu/abt/article/74/9/661/92539/Science-Con-Artists.

Fleury, Theo, et al. Playing with Fire. Triumph Books, 2009.

Gladwell, Malcolm. Blink: The Power of Thinking Without Thinking. Little, Brown and Company, 2005.

Konnikova, Maria. The Confidence Game: Why We Fall for It . . . Every Time. Penguin, 2016.

Shaffer, Howard J. "What is Addiction?" Harvard Health Blog, 10 August 2018, https://www.health.harvard.edu/newsletter_article/how-addiction-hijacks-the-brain.

www.ingramcontent.com/pod-product-compliance
Lightning Source LLC
Chambersburg PA
CBHW070233180526
45158CB00001BA/471